TURKEY
THE
BEAUTIFUL

GERRY CRAWSHAW

TURKEY THE BEAUTIFUL

A Visitor's Guide

W.H. ALLEN · LONDON
1985

Copyright © Gerry Crawshaw 1985

Typeset by Phoenix Photosetting, Chatham
Printed and bound in Great Britain by
Mackays of Chatham Ltd.
for the Publishers W.H. Allen & Co. PLC
44 Hill Street, London W1X 8LB

ISBN 0 491 03761 9

To Paul Ricardo

Contents

Acknowledgements

The author and publishers wish to thank Mr Caglar Yasal and the staff of the Turkish Tourism and Information Office in London for their valuable assistance in the preparation of this book, and for kindly supplying the colour illustrations. The author's special thanks go to Mrs Gülsen Kahraman for her friendship, advice, guidance and inspiration.

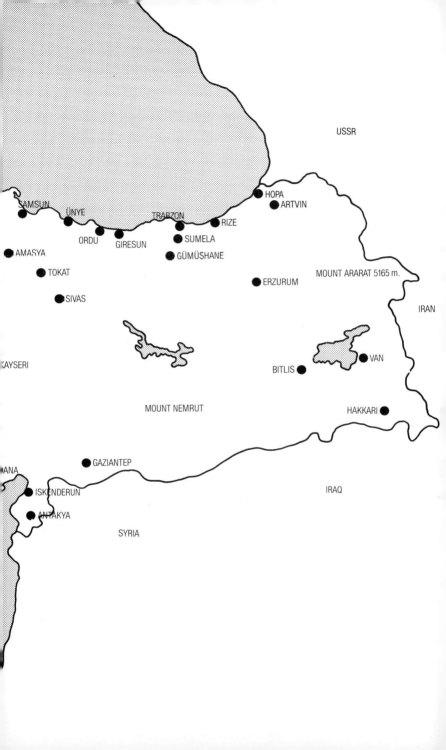

'If you get simple beauty and nought else,
You get about the best thing God invents.'

Robert Browning

One Country, Two Continents –
Introducing Turkey the Beautiful

'If God created so much beauty in the world
it was so that man could enjoy it.'

Mustafa Kemal Atatürk

WITH ITS 8,000 kilometres of coast, beautiful sandy
beaches, picturesque holiday resorts, crystal-clear seas,
impressive scenery, 9,000 years of historical remains,
and its renowned hospitality, Turkey offers the visitor a
truly memorable experience.

From Istanbul, bursting with mosques, opulent
sultans' palaces and a world-famous covered bazaar, to
the holiday resorts of the Aegean, Mediterranean and
Black Sea coasts, through to the rich and fascinating historic sites, troglodyte settlements and underground
cities, Turkey cannot help but amaze and delight.

Yet the country remains relatively 'undiscovered' as a
holiday destination, attracting only about two million
visitors annually from all parts of the world, compared
with the multi-millions of holidaymakers who flock to
many of her Mediterranean neighbours. This can be held
to indicate the country's failure to carve out a place for
herself on the tourist map – but it also demonstrates the
massive opportunities and delights for the traveller in a
country that spans two continents.

The size of Turkey, and its geographical position, have
contributed in no small measure to create problems for

1

the growth of the tourism sector. Transport and communications in many regions are still difficult, although they have been improved greatly over the last decade or so; and the added mileage which separates Turkey from the West – the home of most, but by no means all, tourists – has acted as a deterrent. But this deterrent is more psychological than real, since the cost of travel to Turkey is easily offset by the relatively low cost of living in the country. A meal for two in a good quality restaurant, for example – and it's difficult to find anything but excellent quality in Turkish restaurants, no matter how simple – will cost the visitor less than half what it would in most West European countries.

Over the next few years Turkey expects the numbers of tourists to increase substantially, and there are plans to triple the number of beds in licensed hotels to cope with the demand. This development may be long overdue, but at least it's happening – and happening apace. In particular, great strides are being made in the provision of attractive hotels, holiday villages and tourist facilities at principal Aegean and Mediterranean coastal resorts, although Turkey is trying to avoid building the concrete skyscraper buildings which now blight the coastal fringes of many holiday countries. However, as things stand at present Turkey simply couldn't cope with a major tourism 'explosion'. Local and foreign investment over the past few years has amounted to only about one hundred million dollars a year, and bed capacity is only about 75,000 at present – a figure considerably below that of Tunisia, for example, a country only a fraction of Turkey's size. Although tourism is being given priority by the Turkish government, investors are very slow in coming forward, one of the reasons being that the Turks have traditionally been accustomed to seeing quick returns on operations such as trading, construction and Middle East transport. They are not used to waiting five, ten or even twenty years before recovering their initial investment.

Several grandiose hotel projects, however, are either at

the blueprint stage or in the first phase of construction, especially in Istanbul and Ankara. And with World Bank assistance the delightful Antalya region seems set for a tourist bonanza of substantial proportions. On a less ambitious scale, plans are well advanced to convert the dozens of caravanserais – old stone inns where ancient traders rested and ate free of charge – across the country, into modern-day motels.

It is not just Western visitors that the Turks are catering for. There's a growing influx of visitors from the Middle East, especially Saudi Arabia, and in an attempt to woo Arab investment a new law has been passed making tourism one of the few sectors where 100 per cent foreign ownership is permitted. On the whole, however, the Arabs have been slow to take up the opportunities, although a wealthy Syrian entrepreneur has invested in a project to turn Çandarlı Bay, near Izmir, into a playground for the Arab jet set.

For holidaymakers visiting, or contemplating visiting, Turkey for the first time, what are the recommended resorts and beaches, the most interesting cities and sites? When should they go, and how should they get there? These questions, and various others, I have attempted to answer in the ensuing chapters; but as a quick guide, here are a few suggestions which are obviously subjective but which I hope may be of some assistance.

Recommended Holiday Resorts

Turkey possesses so many uncrowded and uncommercialized holiday resorts that it is obviously difficult to single out a handful which are likely to appeal to the majority. And it needs to be remembered, too, that not all Turkish holiday resorts are 'beach resorts' in the accepted sense, in that the beaches may be on the outskirts of the resort as opposed to the centre. Similarly, the fineness of the sand can vary greatly, from powder to shingle. That said, here are the resorts which I think best cater for the international holidaymaker, with good selections of hotels, restaurants and entertainment facilities, and which are fairly easily accessible:

MARMARIS
Located on Turkey's Aegean coast, Marmaris possesses probably the finest beaches in the country: cove after cove of golden sand fringing a clear, pollution-free sea, making it an ideal family resort. There's a choice of good quality hotels and holiday villages, plenty of facilities for sea sports and no shortage of restaurants; while in the vicinity is a wealth of fascinating historic sites for when you've had enough of soaking up the sun. (See 'The Aegean' section for more details.)

BODRUM
Also on Turkey's Aegean coast, Bodrum is one of my favourite Turkish holiday spots even though it differs from the 'normal' sun-sea-and-sand resort in that there isn't actually a beach where you would expect to find one: that is, in the heart of the town. Instead, the beaches are scattered around the Bodrum peninsula, a short boat-hop or mini-bus drive away from the port itself, and on the doorstep of many of the hotels and holiday villages that fringe the resort. With its lively, youthful and some-what Bohemian atmosphere, excellent fish restaurants and tavernas, Bodrum is a delightful spot, especially for those who appreciate the fun and adventure of searching out for themselves practically deserted beaches in quiet, sheltered coves. (See 'The Aegean' section for more details.)

KUŞADASI
Another port/resort on the Aegean coast, Kuşadası is being increasingly featured in travel company brochures, not only because of its varied attractions, but also because it is a very convenient gateway to some of

Turkey's most impressive historic sites. Like Bodrum, Kuşadası contains a good selection of hotels to suit most budgets, and a choice of excellent restaurants, many located right by the pretty yacht marina. (See 'The Aegean' section for more details.)

SIDE
For those visitors seeking a typical sun-sea-and-sand experience with the bonus of an historic site right on their doorstep – or, in this case, right by the sea – the Mediterranean holiday resort of Side would be my firm recommendation. Not only does the resort have a long stretch of sandy beach, but its picturesque streets bustle with life and are lined with restaurants and tavernas where you can sit and watch the world go by, and with little shops and boutiques piled high with an assortment of handicrafts and souvenirs. And only minutes away from the beach is an impressive historic site, complete with fascinating museum to explore. (See 'The Mediterranean' section for more details.)

There are many other holiday resorts on the Aegean, Mediterranean and the less fashionable Black Sea coasts, the most impressive, in my view, being **Antalya, Alanya, Kemer, Çeşme** and **Fethiye,** but those visitors with time to spare, or who prefer the freedom of touring as opposed to stay-put holidays, could have as much fun and enjoyment as I have had over the years, exploring and discovering for themselves.

Recommended Cities and Towns

Apart from the range of coastal holiday resorts, what of Turkey's numerous and diverse cities and towns? Which ones would a first-time visitor want to see, or a seasoned traveller to re-visit and re-explore?

ISTANBUL

Going to Turkey without spending at least a few days in Istanbul is rather like visiting France and not bothering to see Paris. For some reason Istanbul has acquired the image of being a somewhat forbidding and perhaps even frightening city. In fact, it's a fascinating mixture of East and West, old and new, with a thousand and one riveting sights to keep you engrossed throughout your stay. There's the awe-inspiring and opulent Topkapı Palace, a former sultans' residence; the Blue Mosque, which fully justifies its international fame; the world's largest covered market; and the biggest and most imposing monument to Christianity of its time. True, Istanbul does have something of a 'mysterious' air about it, but this, surely, is hardly surprising when you consider that all around you as you wander through its streets is evidence of three separate and distinct world empires of which Istanbul (formerly Byzantium, later Constantinople) was once the capital.

The visitor to Istanbul should have little trouble making himself understood, or in understanding shopkeepers or restaurant waiters, since most have a smattering of many European languages, and generally a fairly good understanding of English, and they are almost invariably extremely anxious to be helpful.

In short, Istanbul is a city not to be missed if possible, and many travel companies are now making things easier by offering packages combining short stays in Istanbul with a week at one of the popular coastal resorts. (See 'Istanbul' section for more details.)

KONYA

Located in the central Anatolia region of Turkey, and accessible by road from Istanbul and Ankara, Konya is well worth going out of your way to visit, especially, if you can, in December, when the famous Whirling Dervishes' ceremonies are held. Of particular interest in this city is the mausoleum and museum dedicated to the memory of the founder of the Whirling Dervishes, the mystic poet Mevlana. (See 'Central Anatolia' for more details.)

ANKARA
Turkey's capital, Ankara, does not have, for me, the magic and fascination of Istanbul, but is nevertheless a diverting city containing a wealth of interesting buildings, museums and monuments, notably the richly decorated mausoleum of Mustafa Kemal, otherwise known as Atatürk (Father of the Turks), who founded the Turkish Republic and whose vision and influence are still felt in every Turkish village and town. (See 'Central Anatolia' section for more details.)

Recommended Historic Sites

There are so many historic sites located the length and breadth of Turkey that making a selection of 'the best' or 'the most interesting' is virtually impossible. However, here are a few recommendations which, although once again subjective, might nonetheless help point the reader in the right direction – or at least whet his or her appetite for exploration and discovery.

EPHESUS
Of all Turkey's historic sites the magnificent ruins of Ephesus, in the Aegean region, certainly made the most immediate impact on me. Extensive restoration at what was one of the greatest cities of antiquity add to, rather than subtract from, the grandeur and beauty of the city, and the day I made my first walk down Ephesus' famed Marble Road lives with me today as one of those memorable, timeless experiences that happen on but a few occasions in one's lifetime. One can almost sense the presence of the city's long-past inhabitants – and almost hear, or at least imagine, the sound of chariots hurtling down the broad, paved streets.

Ephesus is special in other ways, too, for close by the

site is the tiny house where the Virgin Mary is thought to have spent her last days – a house which is becoming a major centre of pilgrimage for Christians from all over the world. (See 'The Aegean' section for more details.)

CAPPADOCIA
Cappadocia doesn't really classify as a single 'site' but rather a region – a somewhat eerie region, in fact, of amazing houses carved out of soft, volcanic rocks; strange, surrealistic 'fairy chimneys'; rock chapels containing beautiful frescoes; and fascinating underground cities. Excursions to Cappadocia are being featured by a growing number of holiday companies; these are either day trips by coach from Ankara, or sometimes involve a night or two in one of the many new hotels being built to satisfy the tourist demand. (See 'Central Anatolia' section for more details.)

TROY
There isn't as much to see at Troy as at some of Turkey's other ancient sites, but a visit here is nonetheless a memorable experience, if only to rekindle schoolday memories of the well-documented Trojan War. (See 'The Aegean' section for more details.)

PAMUKKALE
There are two treats, not one, in store for visitors to Pamukkale: the unique phenomenon of the staggeringly beautiful petrified waterfalls and not too far away the extensive ruins of Aphrodisias, one of the most impressive archaeological sites in Turkey. (See 'The Aegean' section for more details.)

MOUNT NEMRUT (NEMRUT DAĞI)
Eastern Turkey may not have as much to offer the visitor seeking reasonable hotel comfort as do other regions of Turkey but it does possess one of the most thrilling sites in the country: the gigantic funerary sanctuary erected 2,000 years ago high up Mount Nemrut, and accessible

only by jeep. It's certainly worth all the time and trouble of getting there! (See the 'Eastern Turkey' section for more details.)

THE MONASTERY OF SUMELA
The Monastery of Sumela, dedicated to the Virgin Mary, isn't a 'site' as such, but rather an edifice – and an incredible one at that, perched precariously as it is on a sheer rock face. It is a tourist 'must' if you've got the time. (See 'The Black Sea' section for more details.)

Recommended Itineraries

Turkey is a country of such diverse scenery, climate and historic monuments that, not surprisingly, the traveller is often overwhelmed by the choice of places to visit, especially if he or she is an independent traveller, as opposed to being on a package tour. In order to assist those independent travellers, therefore, here are several suggested itineraries:

TOUR ONE – AEGEAN COAST – 15 DAYS
Spend the first three days exploring Istanbul, on the fourth day depart by ferry boat to Yalova, and then move on to Bursa. On the fifth day visit the sites of Troy and Pergamon and Çanakkale. Spend the sixth day in Izmir. Visit the ruins of Ephesus and Aphrodisias on the seventh day, and spend the eighth day seeing the petrified cascades of Pamukkale. The next three days could be spent in Bodrum, and the twelfth to fourteenth days in Marmaris. Return to Izmir on the last day and then proceed by air or road to Istanbul.

TOUR TWO – CENTRAL ANATOLIA, AEGEAN AND MEDITERRANEAN – 15 DAYS
On the first day, travel to Ankara by air or road. Spend the second day in Konya, seeing the museum devoted to the Whirling Dervishes and the mausoleum of the sect's

founder, Mevlana, and on the third day visit the Central Anatolian valley of Göreme, with its amazing rock tombs and 'fairy chimneys'. On the fourth day visit Kaymaklı and Derinkuyu, with their underground cities, and then on to Mersin and the Mediterranean. The fifth day could be spent between Mersin and Alanya, discovering Korykos and Anamur, and the sixth day in the lively holiday resort of Alanya. On the seventh day visit the beach resort of Side, then Aspendos and Perge, spending the eighth day in Antalya. The ninth day could be taken up visiting Pamukkale, and the tenth Izmir, while the sites of Pergamon, Troy and Çanakkale could be visited on the eleventh day. You could then move on to Bursa for the twelfth day, and spend the remaining three days exploring Istanbul.

TOUR THREE – BLACK SEA, EASTERN AND CENTRAL ANATOLIA – 18 DAYS

Istanbul to Samsun by air on the first day, then along the coastal road to Trabzon, spending the second day exploring this fascinating town. On the third day visit the Monastery of Sumela on the way to Erzurum, where you could spend the fourth day. The following day move on to the frontier city of Kars, and then to Ağrı at the foot of Mount Ağrı. On the sixth day visit Doğubayazıt, and the Palace and Mosque of Ishak Paşa. Spend the next three days by the shores of Lake Van, making an excursion to Akdamar Island. On the tenth day move on to Dıyarbakır and Mardin, and on the eleventh day Urfa and Adıyaman, leaving at 1.00 a.m. on the twelfth day to get to Nemrut Dağı by jeep in time to see the sunrise. Then on to Malatya and Kayseri, spending the thirteenth and fourteenth days among the rock chapels of Göreme. On the fifteenth day move on to Ankara, and then by air or road to Istanbul for the remainder of the visit.

TOUR FOUR – CENTRAL ANATOLIA AND MEDITERRANEAN – 12 DAYS

Spend the first two days in Istanbul, and on the third day

travel by air or road to Ankara. Spend the fourth day in Konya and the next two in Göreme. On the seventh day move on to Mersin and the Mediterranean, spending the eighth day visiting Korykos and Anamur on the way to Alanya. Spend the ninth day in Alanya and visit Side, Aspendos and Perge on the tenth. The next day could be spent enjoying Antalya's attractions, before returning to Istanbul on the last day.

Hints, Tips and Suggestions

TURKISH PEOPLE

Forget the oft-repeated myth that the Turks are un-friendly. The average Turk may look dour, if not actually hostile, but that's an initial impression that doesn't bear scrutiny, certainly not outside the big cities.

Everywhere I've travelled in Turkey I've found the people courteous, open, friendly and, above all, extremely hospitable. On countless occasions at roadside cafés the money I've proffered for a glass of sweet tea or cup of Turkish coffee has been smilingly but firmly refused by generous proprietors seemingly delighted to welcome a foreigner into their midst. It may not be good for business, but it does wonders for international relations! The recent experiences of a friend of mine may also go some way, I hope, towards exploding the equally widely held belief or suspicion that Turkey isn't really safe, especially for the visitor travelling alone. My friend decided to revisit Turkey, alone, in the month of December after having spent a memorable summer holiday in Istanbul and one of the Mediterranean coastal resorts. After reading about, and becoming interested in, the mystic poet Mevlana, founder of the Whirling Dervishes sect, she decided to head for Konya to witness the Whirling Dervish ceremonies held annually at this period. Not only that, but she decided to drive there from Ankara, despite warnings that winters in Central Anatolia can be, and indeed usually are, harsh and severe.

Disregarding friends' cautionary pleas, she flew off to Ankara, picked up a rental car, and proceeded to drive through some of the worst snow storms the villages *en route* had experienced for years. The inevitable happened: the weather became so atrocious that the car eventually ground to a halt. By this time my friend was not only still alone but miles from the nearest major village, and stranded. To the rescue came a family from a tiny village some distance away. Though they didn't speak a word of English – nor my friend a word of Turkish – her problems were obvious, and she was readily welcomed into their home, at considerable inconvenience to themselves. She was soon 'revived' with countless glasses of sweet tea, and later that day entertained to an impromptu folklore performance by a group of hastily assembled village children. When, after a couple of days, the weather improved enough for her to continue her journey to Konya, the village family helped dig her car out of a snow drift before bidding her a fond farewell – having refused all entreaties and pleadings on her part to accept even a small token of gratitude for their hospitality.

The incident may serve to illustrate the foolhardiness and apparent irresponsibility of my friend; it also illustrates the one characteristic for which the ordinary, average Turkish person has every reason to feel proud: a natural and warm hospitality. Of course, offhandedness, rudeness, and crime, exist in Turkey in much the same way as they do in other countries, especially in the big cities such as Istanbul and Ankara. But the myth that Turkish people are ferocious, unfriendly and not to be trusted really is just that: a myth.

MEDICAL TREATMENT

Although treatment is available at all the national hospitals in Turkey – it isn't free, but charges are minimal – visitors would nonetheless be wise to take out insurance before leaving, to cover them in the event of serious illness or accident. Various policies are available, and most can be purchased through travel agencies. In addition to the national hospitals there are also private hospitals and clinics where treatment is much more expensive.

Turkish chemist shops are indicated by the word '*Eczane*' (meaning the place where medicine is sold), or alternatively by '*Apotheke*' or 'Pharmacy', and they stock most of the basic medical supplies the visitor is likely to need.

TIPPING

A service charge of 15 per cent is often added to the bills in most medium-priced and more expensive hotels and restaurants. Where it isn't, a tip of between 10 per cent and 15 per cent is considered appropriate. It has never been customary to tip taxi drivers, because the practice has always been to negotiate the fare before setting off. However, meters are now being widely introduced, so the situation is more confusing, with many drivers expecting a tip in the 10 per cent to 15 per cent range.

VISITING A MOSQUE

Five times a day the *imam* (priest) calls the faithful to prayer in the mosque. Before entering a mosque Moslems wash themselves and remove their shoes. Visitors should also remove their shoes and show the respect they would in any other place of worship. It is also preferable to avoid visiting mosques during prayer time. Women should cover their head and arms, and not wear short skirts; men should not wear shorts.

Istanbul
THE CITY — THE BOSPHORUS —
THE PRINCES ISLANDS

'I am listening to Istanbul, intent, my eyes closed,
The Grand Bazaar's serene and cool,
An uproar at the hub of the Market,
Mosque yards full of pigeons.
While hammers bang and clang at the docks
Spring winds bear the smell of sweat;
I am listening to Istanbul, intent, my eyes closed.'

Orhan Veli Kanık

ISTANBUL IS noisy, overcrowded, bustling, rather dirty –
but, above all, unquestionably one of the world's most
fascinating and exciting cities. I've had the good fortune
to visit Istanbul very many times over the years and the
city has never failed to impress and delight, whatever the
season – perhaps not all that surprising in view of its
amazingly rich and colourful legacy as former capital of
three world empires. Istanbul's strategic setting, bridg-
ing the continents of Europe and Asia and linking the
Black Sea to the Sea of Marmara, has dictated the city's
destiny as an imperial capital for nearly 1,600 years.

Founded 2,600 years ago, the city was made the
Roman capital by the Emperor Constantine and, following the division of the empire, it became a Byzantine
metropolis. Then, in AD 1453, the city that possessed the
mightiest fortifications of the Western world fell to the
Ottoman Turks, led by their tempestuous young sultan,

Mehmet II. Today, Byzantine brilliance and Ottoman opulence blend into this bustling port city, with its great liners at anchor and its little fishing boats bobbing on the waves.

Everywhere, Istanbul's contrasts are apparent, from the sirens of the ships to the timeless sound of muezzins calling the faithful to prayer; from the sunlight flashing off the golden crescent of the domes of the mosques to the hypnotic gaze of Byzantine mosaic figures. The old city is set on a triangular promontory between the Golden Horn and the Sea of Marmara and defended on the landward side by its massive Byzantine walls. Here the Emperor Justinian built Christendom's greatest church, St Sophia. Rivalling the basilica in magnificence is the Mosque of Sultan Süleyman the Magnificent, built by Turkey's greatest architect, Sinan, as well as the Mosque of Sultan Ahmet I, the Blue Mosque, with its six minarets and blue Iznik tiles.

Dominating the city is the mysterious labyrinth of Topkapı Palace, the seat of Ottoman sultans for three hundred years. It was here that the power politics of ruling an empire that stretched from the Gates of Vienna to the Persian Gulf were played out against a background of harem intrigue.

Istanbul has such infinite variety that even a brief visit requires at least three or four days in which to savour its splendours – the ancient churches, palaces and mosques, bazaars and restaurants – and to make at least one unforgettable trip along the Bosphorus, with perhaps a delicious fish lunch on one of the islands.

MONUMENTS, PALACES AND MOSQUES
Topkapı Palace   No visit to Istanbul would be complete without a visit to the amazing Topkapı Palace. Overlooking the Istanbul Boğazı and the Golden Horn, it was the great palace of the Ottoman sultans between the fifteenth and nineteenth centuries. Beside the imposing gate to the palace is the elegant fountain of Sultan Ahmet III. In the first court stands the ancient Church of St Irene, one

of the oldest Christian churches in Istanbul. On the left of
the second court, shaded by cypresses and plane trees, is
the palace kitchen, now housing an exquisite collection
of Chinese porcelain. The Harem, recently beautifully
restored, was the secluded quarters of the wives and con-
cubines of the sultan. It is entered through a gate on the
right side of the court. In the third court is first of all the
Hall of Audience of the sultan, then the library of Ahmet
III. This leads to an exhibition of robes worn by the
sultans and their families, a display of the famous jewels
of the Imperial Treasury, and finally an exhibition of
miniatures. In the fourth court is the Pavilion of the Holy
Mantle, enshrining relics of the Prophet Muhammad.
The palace is open every day except Tuesdays.

Archaeological Museums   These are situated at the
boundary of the first court of Topkapı Palace. The very
rich collection of antiquities in the Archaeological
Museum includes the celebrated Sarcophagus of
Alexander. The Museum of the Ancient Orient displays
antiquities from the Hittite, Assyrian, Babylonian and
Sumerian civilizations. The Çinili Köşk is now the
Museum of Decorated Tiles.

St Sophia (Ayasofya)   This ancient basilica, built by Constantine the Great, is one of the greatest marvels of architecture. Work on St Sophia was begun on Byzantine
Emperor Justinian's orders for the construction of a large
and splendid church; and in AD 535 the building was
opened for worship. Designed by Authemius of Aydın
and the architect Izidor of Milet, the building
immediately earned far-reaching admiration both for the
size of its 32 m. diameter dome and for its dazzling ornamentation.

The basilica underwent repairs in 994. Later it was
looted by European Christians who came to Istanbul
with the army of the Fourth Crusade. According to
accounts of Russian priests who visited Istanbul in the
fifteenth century, St Sophia was in a virtually abandoned

state at that period. In 1453, with the conquest of Istanbul by the Turks, the building was taken over and reorganized. Remains from such ancient cities as Sheba, Ephesus and Baalbek were used in the building's reconstruction and the original walls of St Sophia were decorated with coloured marble and mosaics.

Inside, above the south door of the building – used these days as the main entrance – one's eye is immediately caught by the mosaic in a foundation of gold leaf: here is Mary, sitting on a throne, with the Infant Jesus in her lap and two figures to her left and right. The figure on the left is Constantine the Great, presenting to Mary the city which he founded; and on the right is St Justinian, offering a model of St Sophia. Above the building's actual main door, the Emperor's Gate, is a mosaic portraying Jesus, Mary and the Angel Gabriel. Jesus holds in his left hand a book upon which is written, 'I am the Peace of the World and the Light'. Rampways on four sides of the building lead to the upper galleries. The western side of the top-floor galleries was reserved for the Empress and for the wives of the leading members of the state. In the south gallery there is a section known as the Consul's Meeting Hall. In the middle of the right-hand wall of the hall is a mosaic portraying Jesus, Mary and John the Baptist, while on the east wall are depicted the Emperor Constantine and the Empress Zoe offering to an enthroned Jesus a purse of gold and the imperial edict which ordered the creation of the city.

St Sophia is open to the public every day except Mondays, and there is a café, the Ayasofya, in a quiet corner of the museum's garden in the shade of ancient trees. It is a delightful retreat from the noise and bustle of the city.

The Blue Mosque (Sultan Ahmet Camii) Facing St Sophia is the supremely elegant mosque of Sultan Ahmet I, known as the Blue Mosque because of its magnificent interior decoration of blue Iznik tiles. It is the only mosque to have six minarets. Every evening in summer a *son et lumière* is presented in various languages.

At Meydanı   In front of the Blue Mosque is the site of the ancient Hippodrome, the scene of chariot races and the centre of Byzantine civic life. Of the monuments which once decorated it only three remain: the Obelisk of Theodosius, the bronze Serpentine Column and the Obelisk of Bricks.

Mosaic Museum (Mozaik Müzesi)   The Mosaic Museum was erected to preserve *in situ* exceptionally fine mosaic pavements of the fifth and sixth centuries that remain from the Great Palace of the Emperor of Byzantium. The museum is open every day except Mondays.

Yerebatan Sarayı   To the west of St Sophia is the sixth-century Byzantine cistern known as the Yerebatan Sarayı or Underground Palace. Its chief attraction is its fine brick vaulting supported by 336 Corinthian columns. The underground palace is open every day except Mondays.

Beyazıt Camii   The Mosque of Beyazıt II is one of the oldest mosques in Istanbul (1505). It is surrounded by a complex of religious foundations. The courtyard is beautifully colonnaded and the rare marbles of the sultan's lodge are particularly striking.

Süleymaniye Camii   Standing on the third of the city's seven hills is one of Istanbul's grandest mosques, the Mosque of Sultan Süleyman. Built between 1550 and 1557 by the great architect Sinan, the mosque has four minarets with ten balconies denoting that Süleyman was the tenth Ottoman Sultan.

Türk Ve Islam Eserleri Müzesi   The Museum of Turkish and Islamic Arts is located in the *imaret* (hospice) of the Süleymaniye Mosque. It contains many beautiful Turkish and Persian miniatures, Selçuk tiles, korans and antique carpets. It is open every day except Mondays.

Rüstem Paşa Camii   The Mosque of Rüstem Pasha which stands on the banks of the Golden Horn was built by Sinan on the orders of Rüstem Paşa, the Grand Vizier of Sultan Süleyman the Magnificent. The interior is decorated with beautiful Iznik tiles.

Yeni Camii (1597–1663)   The New Mosque is a familiar sight, located at the Eminönü end of the Galata Bridge. This fine seventeenth-century mosque is preceded by a large courtyard with a particularly elegant fountain for ablution as well as a kiosk decorated with Iznik tiles.

Galata Kulesi (1348)   This huge tower was built by the Genoese in 1348. At a height of 120 m. one can appreciate the lovely panoramic view of the city, the Golden Horn and the Bosphorus.

The Aqueduct of Valens   Built by the Emperor Valens in AD 375, this aqueduct supplied the Byzantine and later the Ottoman imperial palaces with water.

Belediye Müzesi (1946)   The Municipal Museum is located at the foot of the aqueduct in an old *medrese* (theological school) and illustrates daily life in Istanbul. It has displays of costumes and a Turkish shadow theatre. The museum is open every day except the fifth of each month.

Zeyrek Camii   The ancient church of Christ Pantocrator was constructed by the Empress Irene in the early twelfth century. It was later converted into a mosque and is now a museum. The building is open every day except Mondays.

Fatih Camii   Originally built between 1463 and 1470, this mosque of Sultan Mehmet the Conqueror is well noted for its vast complex of annexes including *medreses, imarets* (hospices), hospitals, baths, caravanserai and a library.

Fethiye Camii The ancient church of the Most Blessed Virgin, with its fine fourteenth-century mosaics, dates from the twelfth century. It is open every day except Mondays.

Kariye Camii The eleventh-century church of St Saviour in Chora is, after St Sophia, the most important Byzantine building in Istanbul. It contains a beautiful display of Byzantine mosaics and frescoes of the fourteenth century. The church is open every day except Mondays.

Eyüp Sultan Camii The Great Mosque of Eyüp is the holiest mosque in Istanbul because it is the burial place of Eyüp, the standard-bearer of the Prophet Muhammad, who died in an assault on the walls of the city in AD 670. The mosque and mausoleum were originally built in 1458, but the mosque was rebuilt in 1798.

The Land Walls Built in the fifth century by the Emperor Theodosius II, these walls stretch 7 km. from the Sea of Marmara to the Golden Horn. With their many towers and bastions, they were once the mightiest fortifications in Christendom.

SHOPPING

Kapalı, Çarşı Istanbul is a veritable Aladdin's Cave for visitors who love shopping, browsing or shop-window gazing. There can be few visitors who have not heard of the city's celebrated and vast covered bazaar, the Kapalı Çarşı in the old city, and not surprisingly a visit here is usually high on the list of things to do and places to see in Istanbul.

Personally, I find the stallholders' and shopkeepers' aggressive determination to make a sale a little too overpowering, and tend to avoid the bazaar in favour of the little side streets where there are still plenty of bargains, but without the hassle. However, a visit to the bazaar – especially for the first-time visitor to Istanbul – is an experience not to be missed. But steel yourself against being constantly barracked by over-zealous traders, and be prepared to bargain – loudly and forcefully if necessary.

The bazaar is a labyrinth of shops where each trade has its own street, such as the goldsmiths' street and the carpet-sellers' street. The structure – also known as the Grand Bazaar – grew out of the unification of several historic structures called *bedesten*, which were vaulted and fireproof shopping centres. The Interior Market and the New Market, which make up the largest part of the bazaar, are joined together by fifteen domed vaults. However, this structure is not the whole of the market: numerous commercial buildings, baths, fountains, mosques and shops all form part of the complex. According to records, in the years when the Covered Bazaar was first founded there were 2 markets, 4,399 shops, 2,195 stalls, a bath, a mosque, 10 praying areas, 16 fountains, 2 pools, 8 wells, 25 caravanserais and various supporting structures.

Though times and fashion have changed, there can be no denying that the Covered Bazaar of today offers something to suit practically every taste. There's a tremendous selection of jewellery, for example, from traditional pieces such as harem rings to modern settings. The carpet shops present striking arrangements of carpets and *kilims* (a type of rug) with their vivid colours and intricate designs.

If carpets and rugs are out of your price bracket, there's no shortage of less expensive, traditional Turkish crafts and handicrafts on offer, such as hand-painted ceramic plates, which make stylish wall decorations; hand-made beaten copper and brassware items such as trays, water ewers and cauldrons (but beware of the shoddy, cheaper examples); or perhaps the *heybe* (embroidered bags) and *yastik* (cushions) in the characteristic Anatolian blend of colours. Other items which make excellent souvenirs are vases, bowls and other objects made from beautiful green or gold onyx, and pipes carved out of the soft white meerschaum stone. There are also gaily embroidered blouses in '*şile bez*', an ideal fabric for summer wear from the town of Şile.

Those interested in antiques should head for the Old Bedesten, in the centre of the bazaar, where there's a huge array of authentic antiques and souvenirs: copperware, lamps, armour, jewellery, tiles, silver and glassware.

Mısır Carşısı   Behind the Yeni Camii (New Mosque) is a fascinating bazaar of a different character – the Mısır Çarşısı or Spice Bazaar – where the air is heavy with the aroma from open sacks of mint, thyme, cinnamon and allspice.

Istiklal Caddesi and Cumhuriyet Caddesi   Contrasting with the bustle of the bazaars are the sopisticated shops and boutiques of Istiklal Caddesi and Cumhuriyet Caddesi, both of which lead off Taksim Square. Here one can find elegant jewellery and high-fashion clothing, as well as fine-quality leather goods such as suede coats, jackets and fashionable handbags and shoes.

TRANSPORT
Dolmuş and Taxis   Istanbul doesn't have an underground system, but *dolmuş*, or shared taxis, are a practical and inexpensive means of getting about the city – certainly cheaper than the conventional taxi. *Dolmuş* are recognized by their yellow band, and operate in parts of the city and the suburbs, including areas on both sides of the Bosphorus. Each passenger pays according to the distance travelled and the fares are fixed by the municipality. Main pick-up points are at Taksim, Eminönü, Sirkeci (in front of the railway station), Üsküdar and Kadiköy.

Taxi stations are numerous in the city. Taxis are easily recognized by their chequered black and yellow bands. They have only recently been equipped with meters, but many taxi drivers still ignore these, and it is wise to determine the fare before you move off.

Steamers   These are a practical, enjoyable and cheap means of transport. There are departures from Karaköy (Galata Bridge) to the Bosphorus, the Golden Horn, Üsküdar, Kadiköy, Haydarpaşa (railway station) and the Princes Islands.

Ferry Boats   Ferry boat trips across the Bosphorus from Kabataş to Üsküdar and Sirkeci to Harem operate frequently, and the trip takes between fifteen and twenty minutes.

Trains   There are regular rail departures from Sirkeci station to the beaches on the European side of the Sea of Marmara, and from Haydarpaşa railway station to the beaches on the Asian side.

Buses   On the European side the main bus routes start from Taksim Square, Eminönü Square (near the Galata Bridge) and the Hürriyet Square (near the Covered Bazaar). On the Asian side there are departures from Üsküdar and Kadiköy. There is also a regular, half-hourly bus service from Yeşilköy Airport to the THY Airlines' terminal at Şişhane.

'SECRET' ISTANBUL

Istanbul is one of those cities that doesn't display all its charms in its 'shop window'. In little back-streets and side alleys, away from the main tourist haunts, the visitor can stumble across countless delights. Here are a few of my own discoveries, which I hope you will enjoy as much as I have done.

Kariye   This is one of the very few corners of Istanbul to have survived more or less intact to the present day, although it was subject to considerable neglect and deterioration until quite recently when it was completely restored to its original state. Consisting of a combination of Byzantine and Ottoman buildings, it is located not far from the Edirnekapı Gate, one of the main gates in the old land walls surrounding the city. The famous Byzantine church, with its fourteenth century mosaics and frescoes, is surrounded by a genuinely Ottoman atmosphere. Here you will find a quiet and carefully tended garden where you can relax over tea or coffee.

The square in front of the museum has been closed to traffic, and one corner of this small, historic precinct is now occupied by a building with bookshops and carpet-sellers on the ground floor, and a café serving traditional Turkish sweets on the floor above. The delightful balcony, surrounded by roses, is an ideal place from which to appreciate the attractions of the imposing Byzantine Renaissance museum building.

The Çelik Gülersoy Foundation is housed in another corner of the precinct, in a typical old Turkish house.

Istanbul Market (Cedid Mehmet Efendi Medresesi)
The old Cedid Mehmet Efendi Medresesi, or theological school, is located near the recently restored Konak Hotel, close to Sultanahmet Square. The building had been allowed to fall into ruins, but has now been restored, with its central courtyard converted into a shady garden with trees and flowers. The courtyard is surrounded by a portico with a row of single-celled stone chambers in each of which a master craftsman is engaged on one of the old traditional crafts, such as calligraphy, miniature-painting, marbling or copperwork.

Yıldız Park Yıldız Park forms one of the branches of the great forest that once extended across the whole countryside on the northern shores of the Bosphorus. Until fairly recently the park resembled little more than a neglected wilderness, but in recent years it has been transformed into a palace garden of the nineteenth century. Vehicular traffic has been restricted to a single road, and a network of paths has been created for pedestrians. Stone terraces and platforms have been constructed in shady spots, with old-fashioned benches and wrought-iron lamps. And the neglected patches of coarse grass have been transformed into well-kept lawns.

The Malta Pavilion is the oldest of the buildings in Yıl-dız Park and has been totally restored and furnished in the style of the period. The ground floor and terrace are open to the public as a café, while rooms on the upper floor are available for receptions. The pavilion stands as a model example of the new trend in Turkey towards the appreciation and restoration of old buildings.

The Pink Serra, or Winter Garden, was constructed in 1980 in front of a grove of trees immediately beside the Malta Pavilion. It is nineteenth century in style, and serves both for the display of flowers and as a tea-room for visitors to the park. Everything here is in pink and white: the floor is of pink marble, the lamps hanging from the elliptical ceiling are pink, while the antique plates and decanters arranged in the showcases are wine-coloured – all set against a pure white background. There are marble vases, wrought-iron seats and tables, old-fashioned birdcages. In short, it's a truly delightful place to enjoy morning coffee or afternoon tea.

The Green Serra was constructed in 1983 under high trees in the valley a little beyond the Malta Pavilion. It's in various shades of green, harmonizing with the trees and shrubs and lawns surrounding it. The lanterns suspen-ded from the ceiling are not unlike emerald pendants. One can enjoy refreshments and pastries either in the pavilion itself, or on its shady terrace.

Finally, Yıldız Park boasts yet another delightful terraced café, well known and appreciated by residents of Istanbul themselves but still relatively unknown to holidaymakers – the Çadır, or Tent Pavilion, which was built at the time the grounds were still attached to Çıra-ğan Palace. It was here that Midhat Pasha and his friends faced their first interrogation in 1881. The building was refurbished and opened as a café in 1983. It has a lovely, flower-filled terrace.

Emirgan Park   Emirgan Park forms another corner of the great forest that once covered the slopes along the

Bosphorus. The park itself is first mentioned in the reign of Murat IV, when the Sultan presented the land to the Persian Prince Mir Gun, whom he had brought back with him from his Revan campaign. In the nineteenth century Ismail Pasha built a large wooden palace on the shores of the Bosphorus, as well as a number of pavilions or summer houses in the woodland now known as Emirgan Park but which then formed the grounds of the palace.

Like the pavilions in Yıldız Park, those in Emirgan Park have also been restored and stylishly decorated and furnished to provide tranquil and delightful cafés and tea-houses.

The Pink Pavilion is the oldest of the three buildings in the park, and differs from the other two – the White and the Yellow Pavilions – in being a typical specimen of an old Turkish house in the traditional style. The ground floor now comprises an attractive tea-room, while the various rooms on the upper floor have been furnished in the style of an old Bosphorus Pavilion and opened to the public as a museum and library.

The Yellow Pavilion is in the form of a chalet. It was damaged by fire in 1954 and was subsequently repaired by the municipality of Istanbul before being taken over by the Touring and Automobile Club of Turkey in 1979. The ground floor of the building is now a stylish tea-room, while the terrace in front of the pavilion commands a magnificent view of what must be one of the loveliest sections of the Bosphorus.

The White Pavilion – the third to be erected in the park – is a massive construction in neo-classical style. The building has been restored and converted into a 'Music Pavilion', with its interior decoration and furnishings dominated by light-blue and lilac hues. The larger rooms of the building form a unit now used for the performance of classical music, while the pavilion also boasts collections of books on music and the theatre, a room for the display of various musical instruments, a salon for private meetings and interviews, and a small cinema.

Summer Palace of the Khedive   Another of Istanbul's lesser-known tourist attractions, but one which is well-worth visiting, is the Summer Palace of Khedive, a remarkable building located high in the hills above the Bosphorus and commanding a magnificent view over the blue waters of the straits and the green slopes along each side. The palace was constructed in the first years of the twentieth century. It was completely restored in 1984 and now contains a tea-room, concert hall and lecture rooms and is open to visitors from home and abroad. The style of the building and its furniture reflect the influence of the art nouveau movement.

HOTELS
Istanbul boasts comparatively few international-standard hotels considering the city's size, although there are plenty of smaller establishments, often family-run, offering a reasonable degree of comfort – and usually excellent food. Among the best hotels at the more expensive end of the market are the Hilton, which commands a spectacular view over the city; the Sheraton; the Etap-Marmara in Taksim Square, with its own night-club, Turkish baths and sauna; and the Divan.

The Pera Palas Hotel, built to accommodate passengers on the famous Orient Express, still has its devotees, and is featured extensively in travel companies' programmes. The hotel has been allowed to become somewhat shabby and faded of late, but on my last visit the management promised a massive 'facelift' to restore the building to its original glory. And, faded though the Pera Palas may be, it's still worth dropping in, perhaps for a rakı or tea, just to see the still-magnificent lounge and reception area. Also, you may be able to see the suite of rooms used by Atatürk and now preserved, virtually intact, as a museum.

One of Istanbul's most stylish hotels – and in great demand by the more discerning traveller – is the Konak, an old Turkish mansion located near Sultanahmet Square, between St Sophia and the Blue Mosque. This great mansion had been allowed to fall into neglect and near ruin, but has been carefully restored by the Turkish Touring Club in strict accordance with the original nine-teenth-century plan and façade. It is now a delightful small hotel. There are baths or showers in every room, and the carpets, velvet curtains, old-fashioned brass bedsteads and oil-lamps create a warm and welcoming atmosphere. The hotel's garden contains a monumental pool of porphyry marble and a delightful glass summer-house where teas and snacks are served, all surrounded by flowerbeds under great spreading trees.

RESTAURANTS
There is a huge choice of restaurants in Istanbul, ranging from ones in luxury hotels, with their international and somewhat westernized Turkish food, to the many delightful tavernas lining the Bosphorus and the multi-tude of humbler establishments located on practically every street corner.

Making recommendations is always difficult, especi-ally in a city which boasts such a wide choice, and many visitors will prefer the adventure of discovering favourite places for themselves. But here is a selection of some of Istanbul's better known restaurants; some are more expensive than others but all provide reliable meals at value-for-money prices.

Taksim Square
Divan Restaurant, north of Taksim Square, in the Divan Hotel. Tel. 146 4020
Marmara Etap Hotel, Taksim. Tel. 144 8850

Elmadağ/Harbiye
Bosphorus Terrace Café (Green House), Hilton Hotel. Tel. 146 7050

Osmanbey/Maçka
Çitfnal Farms Restaurant, Samanyolu Sokak No. 8/A, Osmanbey. Tel. 140 7071

Ilyas Steak House, Valikonaği Caddesi (near the intersection with Rumeli Caddesi), Nişantaşı. Tel. 140 3158
Ziya Restaurant, Mim Kemal Öke Caddesi No. 21, Nişantaşı. Tel. 147 1708

Ayazpaşa
Cennet Bahçesi, Sarayarkası Sokağı, Ayazpaşa

Beyoğlu
Çiçek Pasaje, Istiklal Caddesi, Galatasaray. (This is actually a cluster of many tavernas located in the Fish Market.)
The Four Seasons, Istiklal Caddesi No. 509, Tünel. Tel. 145 8941
Galata Tower, Şişhane. Tel. 145 1886

Eminönü
Konyalı Lezzet Lokantası, Mimar Kemalettin Caddesi No. 2 Sirkeci. Tel. 527 1935

Sultanahmet
Konyalı – inside Topkapı Palace. Tel. 626 2727

Beyazıt
Hacıbozanoğulları, Ordu Caddesi No. 214, Laleli. Tel. 528 4492

Kumkapı
Kalyon Restaurant, Ahirkapı Caddesi No. 13. Tel. 526 6250

Along the Marmara towards the Airport
Beyti Lokantasi, Orman Sokak No. 33, Florya. Tel. 573 0963
Florya Et Lokantasi, Florya. Tel. 573 2542
Gelik, Sahilyolu No. 68/70, Ataköy. Tel. 571 3772. (I've enjoyed numerous delightful meals in this busy, unpretentious restaurant that specializes in 'hot well lamb', roasted underground. It's worth going out of your way to sample.)

Hasır, Yeşilyurt Camping, Fener Yolu No. 2 (next to
Çinar Hotel). Tel. 573 8408
Kosova Et Lokantasi, Florya. Tel. 573 1150, 573 7838

Etiler
Şamdan, Nispetiye Caddesi, Etiler. Tel. 168 4898

Along the Bosphorus
Altın Balık Lokantası, Birinci Caddesi, Arnavutköy
Antik, Birinci Caddesi No. 47 Arnavutköy. Tel. 163 6627
(A delightful, antiques-filled restaurant perfect for an
evening meal. A violinist usually entertains.)
Şadirvan, Cevdet Paşa Caddesi (near Bebek Belediye
Gazinosu), Bebek
Abdullah, Mektep Caddesi No. 11, Emirgan. Tel.
163 6406
Canlı Alabalık, Köybasi Caddesi No. 8, Yeniköy

Moda/Bostancı
Koço, Iskele Yanı, Moda. Tel. 336 0797
Dörtler, Kasaplar Çarşısı No. 6, Bostancı. Tel. 358 1958

SUGGESTED ITINERARIES
One-Day Tour   Boarding the boat at the Sirkeci maritime station, sail along the Bosphorus to Sarıyer and see
the Dolmabahçe Palace, Rumeli Fortress and the old
wooden villas on the shores. After lunch return to Sultanahmet Square and visit the Hippodrome, Sultanahmet
Mosque. Yerebatan Sarai and Topkapı Museum. In the
late afternoon visit the Covered Bazaar.

Three-Day Tour   First day: a.m., Tokapı Palace
Museum and St Sophia; p.m., Hippodrome, Yerebatan
Sarayi, Sultanahmet Mosque and Covered Bazaar.
Second day: a.m., Boğazıcı mini cruise; p.m., Süley-
maniye Mosque, Museum of the Ancient Orient, Kariye
Museum, Eyüp Sultan Mosque. Third day: a.m., Rüstem
Paşa Mosque, Archaeological Museum, Spice Bazaar;

30

p.m., Dolmabahçe Palace, Naval Museum, Museum of Painting and Sculpture.

The Bosphorus

A stay in Istanbul should not be completed without the traditional and unforgettable excursion by boat along the Istanbul Boğazı, the winding straits separating Europe and Asia. Along its shores is a delightfully surprising mixture of the past and the present, as well as grand splendour and quaint beauty – modern hotels, ancient wooden houses known as *yalı*, marble palaces and small fishing villages. The best way of seeing the Istanbul Boğazı is to board one of the passenger boats that regularly zigzag up the Bosphorus from the quay at Karaköy. Stopping alternately on the Asian and European side, the excursion takes about seven hours for the round trip. The fare is very reasonable.

The Princes Islands

These nine islands at the mouth of the Gulf of Izmit are famous for their pine-wooded scenery and sandy beaches. They probably take their name from the fact that they were once the pleasure islands of the Byzantine princes. The largest and perhaps most enjoyable of the islands is **Büyük Ada,** an hour's journey by ferry, departing from the Eminönü side of the Galata Bridge.

USEFUL ADDRESSES
Airline Companies
British Airways: Cumhuriyet Cad. 10, Elmadağ. Tel. 148 42 35
KLM: Taksim Square. Tel. 144 46 80
Pan American: at the entrance of the Hilton Hotel. Tel. 147 45 65
SAS: Cumhuriyet Cad. 26, Harbiye. Tel. 146 91 26

Turkish Airlines:
Sales Management, Cumhuriyet Cad. 131 Harbiye.
Tel. 147 13 38, 146 40 17 or 140 23 16
Sales Office Şişhane. Tel. 145 42 08
Sales Office Hilton. Tel. 148 25 04 or 148 39 55
Sales Office Taksim. Tel. 145 24 54 or 145 24 82
Sales Office Sirkeci. Tel. 522 88 88 or 528 48 02
Sales Office Aksaray. Tel. 525 78 81 or 521 46 66
Sales Office Kadıköy. Tel. 335 57 43

Tourism Police
Turizm Polisi, Alemdar Karakolu, Sultanahmet. Tel.
528 53 69

Turkish Maritime Lines
Istanbul Denizcilik Bankası TAO. Tel. 144 02 07

Yeşilköy Airport
Domestic routes: Tel. 573 73 88
International routes: Tel. 573 71 45

Foreign Hospitals
American Hospital, Güzelbahçe Sok, Nişantaşı. Tel.
148 6030
German Hospital, Sıraselviler Cad., Taksim. Tel.
143 55 00
French Hospital (Pasteur), behind the Divan Hotel, Taksim. Tel. 148 47 56
French Hospital (La Paix), Büyükdere Cad., Şişli. Tel.
148 18 32
Italian Hospital, Defterdar Yokuşu, Tophane. Tel.
149 97 51

Rent-a-Car Agencies
Esin, Head Office, Cumhuriyet Cad. 47, Elmadağ. Tel.
143 15 15
Airport Office (international arrivals). Tel. 573 70 24 or
573 29 20, ext. 3326

Kayhan, in the foyer of the Hotel Marmara Etap, Taksim
Square. Tel. 145 07 56 or 145 24 92
Setur, Cumhuriyet Cad. 107, Harbiye. Tel. 148 50 85
Kontur, Cumhuriyet Cad. 283 Harbiye. Tel. 147 95 86 or
147 31 40

Ministry of Culture and Tourism Bureaux
Regional Directorate of Istanbul, Meşrutiyet Cad. 57,
Galatasaray. Tel. 145 68 75, 145 65 93 or 149 27 82
Karaköy Maritime Quay. Tel. 149 57 76
At the entrance to the Hilton Hotel. Tel. 140 63 00 or
140 68 64
Yeşilköy Airport. Tel. 573 73 99, 573 41 36 or 573 20 20
Sultanahmet Square. Tel. 522 49 03
Yalova, Iskele Meydanı 1. Tel. 21 08

Thrace and Marmara

Thrace

THE ROLLING hills and sunflower fields of Thrace comprise the European part of Turkey, cut off from the country's Anatolian heartland in Asia by the Dardanelles, the Sea of Marmara, and the Bosphorus. Standing at the gateway to the East is **Edirne,** ancient Adrianople, the city of Hadrian. Edirne was the first capital of the Turkish Empire in Europe, and was endowed with splendid buildings and monuments: so much so that the town is well worth going out of your way to visit, even though it is all but ignored by tourism bodies and travel firms.

Edirne is a town of attractive cobbled streets lined with ancient wooden houses, and with shops spilling out on to the pavements, offering a multitude of enticements. There are more stalls and shops in the town's bustling bazaar, while also of interest are the Museum of Islamic Art, the Archaeological Museum, with its Roman statues, and the beautifully restored caravanserai of Rüstem Pasha, grand vizier of Süleyman the Magnificent, which was built by Sinan in 1560 and is now a small hostelry for tourists. One of Edirne's most impressive buildings, however, is Sinan's masterpiece the Selimiye Mosque, built between 1568 and 1574 in the reign of Selim II. Its central dome, more than 100 feet in diameter, rests on eight pillars, and the mosque contains a beautiful carved pulpit.

Edirne is also famous for wrestling, and every year, in mid-June, thousands of spectators flock to the annual

Kırkpınar Wrestling Matches, the origins of which date back several centuries. It's quite a spectacle, with the town bursting at the seams with visitors and assuming the atmosphere and air of a medieval fair.

Other places of interest in Thrace include the small town of **Lüleburgaz**, which has several imposing buildings, including the Sokollu Mehmet Paşa Cami, complete with a *hamam* (bath house) and poorhouse; a mausoleum; and a caravanserai.

Marmara

As the demarcation line between East and West, the ancient Marmara region has had a turbulent past. It was from the ancient Abydos that the Persian King Xerxes spanned the Dardanelles with his flotilla of ships; and nearly 2,400 years later these same straits were the scene of General Mustafa Kemal's First World War victory over the Allied forces.

The whole coast of Marmara is lined with sandy beaches, the main resorts being **Yalova,** which is also an important thermal and spa centre, and **Erdek**. The mountainous, forested southern coast of Marmara is particularly beautiful. The highest peak bordering the south coast is that of Uludağ (2,543 metres), and ancient Mount Olympus of Mysia.

At **Gebze**, on the north coast of Marmara, Hannibal lies buried, while a little further down the coast is **Izmit**, the ancient Nicodemia, which for a short period became the capital of the Eastern Roman Empire. A short distance to the south is the town of **Iznik**, which in 1078 passed into the hands of the Seljuks, and in 1331 into those of the Ottomans. From these changes the town has become rich in historic monuments. In the sixteenth century Iznik was famous for the manufacture of tiles, many of which now adorn some of Turkey's most impressive mosques and palaces. The walls surrounding the city, the castle towers and the remains of Roman gates, are evidence of the city's past importance. In 787 the Ecumenical Council was held here in Ayasofya Cathedral, which is still standing to this day. The first domed mosque of Ottoman architecture, the Hacı Özbek Camii; the famous tiled Green Camii; and the Nilüfer Hatun Imareti, are among the impressive Islamic monuments to be seen.

Just outside Iznik the First Crusade came to an end, while it was from **Bursa** that the tiny Ottoman principality expanded to become one of history's greatest empires. Many remains attest to the region's chequered history, from the Roman walls of Izmit and Iznik to the elegant Ottoman buildings of Bursa.

Bursa itself, standing at the foot of Uludağ Mountain, is a meeting place for natural, cultural and historic riches. The town takes its name from Prusias I, King of Bythinia, and is embellished with many very early examples of the architecture of Ottoman culture. A visit to this green and pleasant town – Turkey's sixth largest with a population of over a million – should begin at the Green Mausoleum: located in the eastern part of the town, in the midst of an attractive garden, it is decorated with blue-turquoise and green octagonal tiles. Nearby is an archaeological museum displaying remains from Roman and Byzantine architecture and an interesting coin collection. Further to the east is Emir Sultan Camii, while proceeding through a quarter rich with attractive old houses one reaches Yıldırim Beyazit Camii, one of the first mosques in the Ottoman style. From here, turning to Cumhuriyet Square, the town centre, one reaches the covered market with its caravanserai and *bedesten*, while further on is the dome-shaped Ulu Camii, the biggest in Bursa. Inside, the fountain, carved walnut pulpit and rich calligraphic decorations, are of particular interest. Finally, one should not miss the very impressive blue-tiled Muradiye Camii, located next to a pretty garden which in summer is ablaze with roses and magnolia blossoms. In the garden is the tomb of Murat I and his family.

In addition to its impressive selection of magnificent

buildings, Bursa is also renowned as one of Turkey's major health and spa resorts. The thermal baths are situated mostly in the Çekirge district, the most important of them being Kocamustafapaşa, Vakıf Bahçe, Kaynarca, Kürkürtlü and Çelik Palas. Many of the baths are contained within some of Bursa's most historic and interesting buildings, often former bath houses. The spa waters themselves contain bicarbonate, sulphate, sodium, calcium and magnesium, are used for bathing and drinking treatments, and are said to be beneficial in the treatment of diseases relating to rheumatism, gynaecological ailments, skin, post-operation fatigue, and disorders of the metabolism.

PLACES OF INTEREST NEARBY
No visit to Bursa should be completed without an ascent of **Uludağ** – especially if you visit the town in springtime, when the plain below the mountain is a beautiful green, and the hillsides are ablaze with blossoms and wild flowers. A cable car operates from the hillside to the east of the town, or one can take a taxi up the mountain road from Çekirge. The view from the top is magnificent.

West of Bursa is **Karacabey Hara**, a government-operated stud farm for thoroughbred horses, while the resorts of **Gemlik, Mudanya** and **Yalova** are all quite accessible.

HOW TO GET TO THRACE AND MARMARA
By Road   There's a reasonably good road from Istanbul (E5) to Thrace, and buses operate to both Edirne and Bursa from all major Turkish cities. Alternatively, you can fly to Bursa from Istanbul.

By Train   The Marmara Express operates between Izmir and Bandırma, with connecting links.

By Boat   There's a frequent hovercraft service from Istanbul to Yalova, Armutlu and Mudanya.

USEFUL ADDRESSES
Tourism Bureaux
Edirne: Londra Asfaltı, No. 48. Tel. 1490-5260
Bursa: Atatürk Cad. No. 82. Tel. 12359

Turkish Airlines
Bursa: Cemal Nadir Cad. 8/A. Tel. 21866

The Aegean
IZMIR — TROY — PERGAMON — ÇEŞME — KUŞADASI — EPHESUS — PRIENE — MILETOS — DIDYMA — BODRUM — MARMARIS — DATÇA — FETHIYE — PAMUKKALE — APHRODISIAS

'Tell me, Muse, of the man of many tricks who wandered far and wide after he had sacked Troy's sacred city, and saw the towns of many men and knew their minds.'

Homer

TURKEY'S LOVELY Aegean coastline is magnificently for-med, lapped by the clear waters of the Aegean and abounding in extensive sandy beaches, rocky bays and wooded shores. There are numerous centres of attrac-tion, ranging from the modern, lively metropolis of Izmir to the picturesque port of Ayvalık, with its rocky shores and pinewoods; Kuşadası, overlooking a lovely bay and surrounded by sandy beaches; Bodrum, with its pretty white houses grouped behind the medieval castle; and the red roofs of Marmaris, nestling along the shores of a fjord-like bay with limpid blue waters, and boasting some of the best beaches in Turkey.

Not only endowed with great natural beauty, the region is rich in historic sites: Troy and Pergamon to the north of Izmir; and Ephesus, Priene, Miletos and Didyma to the south. Further inland are the remarkable remains

of Aphrodisias, and the ruins of Hierapolis next to the
fascinating petrified cascades and thermal pools of
Pamukkale.

Izmir

Turkey's largest port and her third largest city, Izmir is
impressively situated at the end of a large gulf ringed by
mountains. Although not a holiday resort in the true
sense of the word, it is a good base for exploring some of
Turkey's most impressive sites, or an intermediate stop
on the way south.

The bay is dotted with ships and there is always a fresh
sea-breeze blowing across this modern city, with its
palm-lined avenues and lively atmosphere. There are
few vestiges of Izmir's rich past, owing to the great fire
that destroyed much of the city in 1922. However, there
are still many places of interest well worth visiting.

If you leave from Cumhuriyet Meydanı (Republic
Square), where there is an imposing statue of Atatürk,
you can walk along Atatürk Caddesi, which runs along
the sea front and is lined with restaurants, night-clubs
and travel agencies. At Konak Meydanı there is an
elegant clock-tower in the Moorish style. From here you
can walk through the little streets to the bazaar, which is
always lively and colourful. Close to the bazaar are three
attractive mosques, the Kemeraltı Camii, Hisar Camii
and Şadırvan Camii, plus two seventeenth-century caravanserais.

Not far from the bazaar are the imposing remains of the
Roman agora, dating from the second century AD.
Several portals lead on to the square, where you can see
the beautiful statues of Poseidon, Demeter and Artemis.

Kadifekale, the Velvet Castle, dominates the city from
the top of Mount Pagos. It was on this mountain that,
according to legend, Nemeses appeared to Alexander the
Great in a dream and told him to found a city on this site
and encourage the inhabitants of the old city of Izmir to

move here. The original fortress was constructed by Lysi-machus, one of Alexander the Great's generals, and it was later restored by the Romans and the Byzantines. From the castle there is a magnificent panorama of the city and the bay of Izmir.

Thanks to its excellent range of hotels – including the impressive Büyük Efes Hotel – and transportation facilities, Izmir is an ideal point for departure for many excursions, including Pergamon and Ephesus and, for those using Izmir as a base, further afield to Çeşme, Manisa and Sardis. All the Izmir travel agencies organize frequent excursions to Ephesus and Pergamon.

SHOPPING IN IZMIR
Many beautiful carpets, both antique and modern, can be obtained in the region. Carpets made in such famous centres as Bergama, Uşak, Gördes and Milas can be found in Izmir's bazaar and in shops in the centre of the city.

Most of Izmir's shops are along Atatürk Caddesi on the sea front. Look out for local handicrafts such as jewellery, copperware, and suede and leather garments.

USEFUL TELEPHONE NUMBERS
Turkish Airlines (THY)
Büyük Efes Hotel Agency. Tel. 14 12 20

Turkish Maritime Lines
Yeni Liman, Alsancak. Tel. 13 74 81

Tourism and Information Bureau
Atatürk Cad. 418, Alsancak. Tel. 21 68 41 and 22 02 07

Troy

There can be very few readers for whom the name Troy does not immediately fire the imagination. The account of the Trojan war by Homer, the blind poet from Izmir, made the name of this Turkish city famous, and at the end of the nineteenth century Schliemann, an amateur archaeologist, discovered the site at a place called Hisarlık, located near the confluence of the Dardanelles and the Aegean Sea. Troy, of course, existed long before the Trojan War and remained long after: in fact, the excavations revealed nine principal levels of occupation dating from the end of the Chalcolithic period until the Roman period, and the long history of the city extends over 4,000 years. A visit to the site reveals the ruins of the impressive ancient fortifications of Troy VI (the city of Priam, destroyed around 1250 BC); the towers of Troy I, one of which is in a well-preserved state; the paved ramp to the gate of Troy II; as well as a theatre and bouleuterion of the Roman period. The small local museum is well worth visiting.

Çanakkale, a port situated at the narrowest part of the Dardanelle Straits, is a convenient point of departure for a visit to Troy. The town was developed around the fortress that was built in 1452 by Sultan Mehmet II, and today one can visit the fortress and the museum.

From Çanakkale there are maritime connections with Istanbul, and nearby is the resort of **Intepe**, with an attractive beach fronted by pine woods. A few kilometres away is **Behramkale**, a fishing village standing on the site of the ancient city of Assos, which was built by the Aeolians around the first millennium BC. On the acropolis lie the ruins of the famous Temple of Athena, which was probably built during the sixth century BC, and from the top of the acropolis there is a panoramic view of the sea and the Greek island of Mytilene, also known as Lesbos.

Pergamon

There is an excellent road (105 km.) that links Izmir with Bergama, the ancient Pergamon, capital of the Pergamese kingdom from the third century BC and one of the most brilliant Hellenistic cultural centres. In 133 BC, on the death of the last Pergamese king, the kingdom was taken over by the Romans. The extensive ruins give some impression of the former might of this city that rivalled Alexandria and Antioch as a centre of the arts and sciences.

The city is divided into three parts: the Acropolis, or upper city, set impressively on a high hill; the middle city; and the Roman, lower city.

A visit to Pergamon should begin in the lower city with the Asclepieion, one of the foremost medical centres of the ancient world, dedicated to the cult of Aesculapius, the Roman god of medicine. The huge complex includes temples, treatment rooms, pools, a sacred spring, a library and even a theatre for entertainment. The famous Roman surgeon Gallen worked here, and the Roman emperors Marcus Aurelius and Caracalla came here for cures. A range of treatments was provided, from mud baths to sacred drinking water. The priests also employed psychological techniques, making patients run down tunnels to listen to what they believed were encouraging messages from the gods but which were, in fact, messages shouted by the priests themselves through holes in the tunnels' roofs.

On the main road that passes through Bergama there is the Archaeological Museum, housing Hellenistic and Roman works of art, as well as some fine terracotta figurines from Myrina. Also in the town are the interesting Ethnographical Museum, the Ulu Cami (Great Mosque), a Seljuk minaret and the ruins of the large Kızıl Avlu (Red Courtyard), which is a Byzantine basilica built over the site of a temple dedicated to the Egyptian god Serapis.

A steep, 3 km. road takes you to the top of the Acropolis, built in the Hellenistic period. There are triple fortifications enclosing the royal palace, temples, houses and shops. Opposite the main gateway of the Acropolis stands the famous library of Pergamon, built by King Attalos I. The library contained 200,000 books, which were transferred to Alexandria as Mark Antony's gift to Cleopatra. All these parchment manuscripts were lost when the library at Alexandria burnt down in the fourth century AD.

Close to the library is the Temple of Athena, in the Doric style, and nearby is the breathtaking theatre, set in a deep escarpment. To one side of the theatre are the Temple of Trajan and the Temple of Dionysus, and to the other side are the ruins of the huge Altar of Zeus. The magnificent frieze from this altar, depicting the battle of the Giants and the Gods, is now in the Berlin Museum.

From the Altar of Zeus you can descend to the middle city via the upper agora. In this section of the city are the Temple of Demeter, the huge gymnasium and the lower agora.

On your return from Bergama to Izmir it is worth stopping at the interesting little village of **Aliağa**, built out of materials taken from the ancient Aeolian city of Kyme; and at **Foça**, the ancient Phokala, whose inhabitants founded such Mediterranean cities as Marseilles, Antibes and Nice. Today Foça is a pretty little port where you can see the ruins of a Genoese fortress.

Çeşme

The little port of Çeşme, situated at the tip of the peninsula stretching to the west of Izmir, is a resort and thermal centre, a long-time favourite of Izmir residents and only fairly recently 'discovered' by foreign tourists and yachting enthusiasts.

The resort crouches at the foot of a mighty, well-preserved fifteenth-century fortress. Nearby, the thermal spa of Ilıca is located behind an extensive sandy beach, constantly refreshed by a sea breeze called the Imbat. The coast between Ilıca and Çeşme is dotted with numerous hotels and an extensive holiday village. Yachtspeople have a choice between the little ports of Çeşme, Dalyan, Ilıca and the very new harbour at the Golden Dolphin Holiday Village.

The thermal springs of Çeşme are reputed to be an

effective treatment for rheumatism, while between Izmir and Çeşme there are a number of other thermal springs: the Bath of Agamemnon, some 10 km. from Izmir; the springs of Urla (purgative waters with a magnesia-salt base) and those of Güzel-Bahçe.

In ancient times Çeşme, or Kysus as it was then known, was one of the most important cities of Ionia and it has been an important medical treatment centre and an active travel and naval base for centuries. Twenty-two kilometres north-east of Çeşme, at **Ildır**, are the ruins of Erythrai, another of the important Ionian cities. Founded on the coastline of a beautiful bay dotted with small islands, Erythrai was inhabited by Cretans and Pamphylians after the wars of Troy and, although the people managed to hang on to their traditions, the city became part of the Ionian parliament. However, it was overthrown by Basili de Genos, and later Ortyge's tyranny began. Erythrai had to struggle against Kios, who claimed trade monopoly, and the attack of the Persians brought an end to the disagreements and caused Erythrai's collapse.

Today, Çeşme and its surroundings survive on tobacco, olives, aniseed, citrus fruits and grape cultivation, and fishing – and, increasingly, on tourism. One of the biggest holiday developments in the whole of Turkey is located here: the vast, Golden Dolphin Holiday Village. This 'resort within a resort' boasts three hotels offering, at the last count, more than 550 rooms, two table d'hôte restaurants with Turkish and French specialities, and an à la carte restaurant. Facilities include shops, health studio, sauna, hairdressing salon, tennis courts, swimming pools, playground and separate pool for children, as well as a yacht marina. Sea sport activities available include diving, fishing, water-skiing and windsurfing, and instruction is also available in tennis, water-skiing and horseback riding.

Çeşme itself is a somewhat sprawling resort, the word being used to describe the western part of the Peninsula of Urla, an area of 260 sq. km., with Ilıca as its most popular tourist centre. The Çeşme area has an extensive range of hotels and pensions, many with their own thermal springs, while the shallowness of the sea water makes Çeşme a popular holiday resort for families with young children.

HISTORIC SITES

Fortress of Çeşme   The fourteenth-century Genoese fortress was enlarged, and new towers added, during its restoration in 1508 by the Ottoman Sultan Beyazıt II. The fortress had been constructed beside the sea, but the sea was later filled in by the coast, as can be seen today. The castle and the port provided protection for the trading ships and the navy against inclement weather and enemy attacks. According to an inscription on the inside gate, the little mosque was built during a restoration by Beyazıt II, son of Mehmet the Conqueror. The minaret, which had become a ruin, was rebuilt in the nineteenth century but was later destroyed by an earthquake. The south gate of the fortress is a characteristic example of Ottoman architecture.

Museum of Ottoman Arms   Located inside the fortress, this exhibition of cannons, swords, armour, pistols and rifles was opened in 1965. Most of the exhibits were gathered from collections at the museum of Topkapı Palace, Istanbul. A gold- and silver-encrusted rifle, once belonging to Sultan Abdulaziz, is a prize exhibit.

Caravanserai   Built in 1529 by architect Omar, this two-storey inn is a typical Ottoman caravanserai. Around the wide courtyard are shops, warehouses and various rooms.

Mausoleum   This eighteenth-century hexagonally designed mausoleum reflects the main characteristics of Ottoman mausoleum architecture.

Mosques   Two of Çeşme's nineteenth-century

mosques, Hacı Memiş Camii built in 1832 and Hacı Mehmet Camii in 1842, are still in use.

Hunting Çeşme has built up a reputation as a centre for hunting – in particular, boar hunting. The area is also a good centre for partridge and hare shooting, especially during the months of September through to December – but licences are required.

USEFUL TELEPHONE NUMBERS
Tourism and Information Bureau: Iskele Meydani No. 8. Tel. 66 53

PLACES OF INTEREST NEARBY
A detour from the Izmir–Çeşme road to Şeferihisar leads to the village of **Sığacık**, a picturesque little port surrounded by fortified walls dating from the Genoese period. To the west of the Bay of Sığacık is an attractive beach from which the site of ancient **Teos** is easily accessible: the wooded site is pleasant and tranquil and the remains of the famous Temple of Dionysus and an odeon are still visible. Quite near the site is the delightful beach of **Akkum.**

Kuşadası

Kuşadası, meaning the 'Island of Birds', is a lovely little port nestling along the shores of a glittering bay around a tiny islet covered in flowers. Not surprisingly, it has become one of the Turkish Aegean's most popular holiday spots and a particular favourite with British holidaymakers. What has increased its popularity is its comparative proximity to Izmir – about two hours by road – and to some of the best archaeological sites in the Aegean, notably Ephesus.

It is a terraced village overlooking what many consider to be the most beautiful bay of the Aegean and it seems to have been created purely for the delight and pleasure of the holidaymaker, with its old caravanserai – now a stylish hotel complete with a very attractive courtyard restaurant – white minarets, shady terraces where one can sit and sip rakı and eat grilled fish, and a main street lined with little shops offering a thousand and one tempting bargains.

On the little isle known as **Güvercin Adası** (Isle of Doves), now joined to the mainland by a small jetty and standing amidst a forest of flowers, is a small fortress built by the Turks in the fourteenth or fifteenth century and said to have been a den of the famous Barbaros Brothers, whose daring escapades were known throughout the Mediterranean. Today, the surrounding gardens and discothèque inside the castle are the haunt of ever-increasing numbers of tourists, especially in the evenings.

A brand-new yacht marina, which is being extended ever further, lies behind the main harbour where cruise liners are frequently berthed.

There are excellent beaches in the immediate environs of Kuşadası: **Içmeler**, on the road to Selçuk; **Kadınlar Denizi** (Women's Sea); and **Yavansu** and **Güzelçamlı.**

Ephesus

The magnificent ruins of Ephesus, one of the greatest cities of antiquity and the Roman capital of Asia, lie 75 km. to the south of Izmir and about fifteen minutes by road from Kuşadası. Ephesus is a reflection of imperial might and Western opulence. It was from here that the elegant Ionian settlement changed hands many times, passing to the Lydian King Croesus; the Persian King Cyrus; Alexander the Great; the kings of Pergamon; Mithradates, King of Pontus; and the Romans. Ephesus reached the apogee of its prosperity during the period of peace and intense commercial activity in the Roman Empire in the second century AD.

The city was the centre of the cult of Artemis, the

Roman Diana, daughter of Zeus and goddess of the hunt and chastity, who was identified in Asia Minor with Cybele, the 'universal mother' and symbol of fertility. It was St Paul who aroused the animosity of the Ephesians by preaching against the cult. In the same period the Virgin Mary is believed to have spent her last days in Ephesus, accompanied by St John. The mother-cult of the Virgin eventually supplanted that of Artemis and it was in the Double Church of the Virgin in Ephesus that the dogma of the Virgin Birth was laid down in AD 431.

A full day is necessary to see all the treasures of Ephesus. You can begin your tour with a visit to the little town of **Selçuk**. Just outside of here lie the remains of one of the Seven Wonders of the World, the Temple of Artemis. Unfortunately only the foundations remain of this magnificent temple, built in Alexander the Great's time, after the archaic temple was burnt down by Herostratus. Not far from the Artemision is the Isa Bey Mosque, built by the Seljuks in the fourteenth century; it has a beautiful marble portal.

At the top of the hill is the citadel and the Basilica of St John, built by the Byzantine emperor Justinian in the sixth century on the alleged site of the tomb of the apostle. In the town you should not miss the Archaeological Museum, which houses many beautiful works of art found at Ephesus, including the famous statue of Artemis and the bronze of a boy and a dolphin.

Three kilometres from Selçuk, on the road to Kuşadası, a road branches off to Ephesus, set at the foot of Panayır Dağı (Mount Pion). To the left of the entrance to the site there is the Vedius Antonius Pius. Opposite the gymnasium is the monumental portal of the Stadium of Nero and, close by, the ruins of the Double Church of the Virgin, where the Ecumenical Councils of AD 431 and 449 were held.

To the left of the church is the Arcadian Way, a colonnaded marble way that led to the ancient harbour. At one end of the Arcadian Way is the great theatre, recently restored, which can accommodate 25,000 people. It was in this theatre that St Paul preached against Artemis, and today the theatre is still used for folkloric performances during the Ephesus Festival.

Leading off from the theatre is the Marble Road, lined with monuments. To the left of the Marble Road is the Curetes Street, lined with villas, statues and fountains. Along this street you can see the elegant façade of the Temple of Hadrian, the Baths of Scholastika and the monumental Fountain of Trajan. Beyond the fountain is the Prytaneion, the town hall and the State Agora. To the north of the Magnesian Gate is the Roman gymnasium, while about one kilometre from the gate is the Grotto of the Seven Sleepers, where seven young Christians are said to have slept for 200 years to escape persecution.

House of the Virgin Mary   At the summit of Bülbül Dağı (Nightingale Mountain), 7 km. from Selçuk, is a humble Byzantine chapel on the site of the house where the Virgin Mary is said to have spent her last days. The house was discovered following the description of a German visionary nun in the nineteenth century. The place is recognized by the Vatican as Mary's last home and in 1967 Pope Paul VI honoured it with a visit. Today, the simple chapel attracts many thousands of pilgrims each year and a special Mass is celebrated on the 15 August.

Priene

Priene was one of the busiest ports of the Ionian Federation. What makes the site of particular interest is the system of geometric planning introduced in the fourth century BC by Hippodamos of Miletos. The theatre is Priene's most interesting remain; the lower tiers are virtually intact and the whole theatre retains its original character. Only a few columns remain of the Temple of Athena, which was a classic example of Ionian architecture.

Miletos (Milet)

Miletos, like Priene, was a great Ionian port and the native city of several philosophers and sages. Most of the monuments at the site are badly ruined except for the theatre and the baths of Faustina. The theatre, reconstructed during the Roman period, is an impressive building.

Didyma (Didim)

Didyma possesses only a single monument – but it is, nevertheless, a marvellous site. The Temple of Apollo was one of the most sacred places of antiquity and, despite being looted and burned many times, it is still impressive.

Bodrum

Dominated by a medieval castle, the picturesque port of Bodrum is one of Turkey's most popular holiday resorts – and it is an enchanting place, even at first sight. Though capital of several ancient civilizations, in more recent times Bodrum was simply a small sponge-fishing town that few outsiders had heard of. But thanks to its lovely climate and the hospitality of its people, this little resort has leapfrogged into the limelight of tourism. With its bay bordered by white villas and palm trees, its busy harbour with elegant yachts built by the carpenters of Bodrum, its fun-loving residents and their easy-going, almost Bohemian life-style, and a wide range of excellent hotels and self-catering apartments and villas, its growing popularity is easy to understand.

Bodrum – ancient Halicarnassus – was capital of a region called Caria, whose original inhabitants were of an origin so old as to be unknown. They may even have been related to the Minoans of Crete. After 1200 BC a series of migrations began to settle in the area, and the immigrants' first settlement was a fortress in the area of the present-day Bardakçi. The original inhabitants tended to build on the summits of the surrounding hills.

In the seventh century BC Halicarnassus joined the Dorian League – a confederation of cities including Kos and the three Rhodian cities of Kamiros, Lindos and Ialyos – but was expelled after an argument. At the time Halicarnassus was known for its olives, oil, figs, wine and honey. During the middle of the sixth century BC Halicarnassus was conquered by the Persians. The famous Artemisia I, daughter of Lygdamis, became ruler and sailed with the Persians against Athens as Admiral of the Fleets of Halicarnassus, Kos, Nissiros and Kaliymnos – and showed such courage that Xerxes is claimed to have said that all of his admirals should have been women!

After Artemisia I, Lygdamis II came into power and during his reign Herodotus, known as the 'Father of Modern History', was exiled (484 BC). After travelling round the known world and producing a voluminous work, Herodotus returned to Halicarnassus to help over-throw Lygdamis II.

In 387 BC Hecatomnus of Milassa became satrap and Milassa was made capital of Caria. His son Mausolus moved the capital back to Halicarnassus and became an independent ruler, establishing a Carian Empire. He was an able and enlightened man. When he died young, his wife and sister Artemisia II began building his tomb, which was finished after her death and became one of the Seven Wonders of the Ancient World and gave us our modern word 'mausoleum', meaning ornate tomb.

Artemisia II ruled for two years, defeating and destroy-ing the Rhodian fleet. After her reign the satrapy passed back to Persia and, in 334 BC, in his conquest of the world, Alexander the Great defeated and razed the city. The ruins were part of the dominion of Antigonus, the Lysi-machos, later the Selucuids and, finally, at the end of the third century BC the empire fell to the Ptolemies.

In AD 190 Halicarnassus was made a free city by the

Romans and a little later was placed under Rhodian domination. In the fourth century AD it became part of a Christian archbishopric with the capital of Aphrodisias. Between the fourteenth and fifteenth centuries the Seljuk Turks and the Byzantines passed the Carian area back and forth between them.

In 1402 the Knights of Rhodes landed in Bodrum and, using the stone columns of the mausoleum, built a castle to St Peter on the site of the Dorian acropolis and a Seljuk castle. The knights tried hard to protect their position, even installing several cannons, but 120 years after their arrival Süleyman the Magnificent, after defeating the Knights of Rhodes, sailed towards Bodrum in 1523, and the Knights of St John surrendered and moved west to Malta, where their order still exists today.

Bodrum Castle   The castle, which is one of Bodrum's principal attractions, is open to the public. The five towers, built by the Knights of Rhodes according to their nationality – French, Italian, German, Spanish and English – and the Gothic chapel have all been carefully restored. The English Tower has been furnished with reproductions of tapestries, furniture, weapons and armour of the fifteenth century, giving the visitor an excellent idea of the life of those times. The courtyards of the castle are adorned with plants and trees, and statues and amphorae form an open-air museum. The French and Italian Towers and the Gothic Chapel are used as archaeological museums, displaying objects taken from sites around Bodrum. And the best known of the museums, that of Underwater Archaeology, contains very valuable objects recovered since 1968 from expeditions in the Aegean and Mediterranean Seas. There are pieces of the hull and parts of the cargo of a Byzantine ship that sank about AD 620; the wreck of a Bronze Age ship which went down about 1200 to 1300 BC; and the wreck of an Islamic ship which was loaded with glass.

The ancient theatre on a hill behind the mausoleum, though not yet completely excavated, offers a magnificent view of the modern resort of Bodrum.

PLACES OF INTEREST NEARBY

Holidaymakers who choose Bodrum as a base for exploring the region will certainly not be disappointed, since there is a host of interesting excursions possible that will embrace the delightful countryside, unspoiled beaches, charming villages and fishing ports.

Bardakçı Bay (Salamakis) is the nearest beach to Bodrum, just ten minutes away by boat. Here one can visit the fountain of Salamakis, named after a nymph who fell in love with Hermaphrodite, son of Hermes and Aphrodite. When the young god did not return the nymph's love, Zeus took pity on her and combined her body and that of her beloved into one. Today, Bardakçi is a pretty little bay, complete with small pensions, restaurants and even a discothèque overlooking a crystal-clear sea.

Gümbet is a small bay about 3 km. outside Bodrum, offering sandy beaches surrounded by citrus orchards. There are many good small hotels, camp sites and restaurants.

Bitez is about 8 km. from Bodrum and has a bay, pleasant hotels, restaurants and cafés. It is a picturesque village, set in citrus groves.

Yalıkavak, a fishing hamlet at the end of a deep gulf, Yalikavak can be reached by taking a right turn off the Karatoprak road and proceeding along a road that offers magnificent views of both sides of the Bodrum Peninsula. The small settlements adjoining Yalıkavak are reknowned for the quality of their woven kilims (rugs).

Ortakent is a charming village 13 km. from Bodrum, lying at the foot of hills and surrounded by windmills. The village itself boasts some interesting old fortress houses, while 2 km. further along a tree-shaded lane are attractive beaches and pleasant small hotels.

Gölköy is a little village set among trees and gardens, with a selection of small hotels and restaurants; it is noted for its cool breezes even on the hottest day. To the right of the bay are the ruins of an ancient settlement.

Gümüşlük, a picturesque fishing village near the ancient port of Myndos, is located about 25 km. from Bodrum. Sites include the ruins of a city wall and a Byzantine church.

Turgut Reis, a fishing village 20 km. from Bodrum, has one of the finest sandy beaches in the area, as well as a good selection of small hotels and restaurants.

Torba, lying 8 km. north of Bodrum, is one of the most productive fishing bays on the peninsula. There is good seafood at the small cafés and restaurants by the sea.

Also along the peninsula are the small villages and settlements of **Türkbükü, Gündoğan, Akyarlar, Bagla, Karaincir** and **Kargı,** offering secluded swimming, quiet local cafés and freshly caught fish.

DAILY BOAT TRIPS
Daily boat trips from Bodrum are among the highlights of a visit to this resort. You can either rent a boat privately or join a tour and have the opportunity to meet other people. One of the most impressive sea trips from the resort is the famous Blue Voyage, a cruise in the Gulf of Gökova, a large bay east of Bodrum. This offers a constantly changing coastline, with wooded coves, rocky cliffs, sandy beaches, mysterious land-locked fjords and small farming settlements.

PLACES OF ARCHAEOLOGICAL INTEREST IN GÖKOVA
Ören, formerly known as Ceramos, is an ancient settlement. Some city walls, gates and a temple foundation survive.

Sedir Island is probably a Hellenistic site. There are well-preserved walls, towers, remains of a Temple to Apollo (later a church) and a well-preserved theatre. Cleopatra is said to have visited here with Mark Antony; sometimes this island is called Cleopatra's Island. Its white sandy beaches are a feature.

Knidos is another ancient site, still being excavated. Attractions include two ancient harbours, commercial to the east, military to the west, as well as the remains of the theatre, Temple of Aphrodite, city walls and a cemetery. There are pleasant cafés specializing in fresh fish.

FERRY BOATS TO KOS
Every Monday, Wednesday and Friday in the summer season there are Turkish boats sailing from Bodrum to the Greek island of Kos. They leave Bodrum in the morning and return in the afternoon.

SHOPPING IN BODRUM
Bodrum's lively outdoor market operates on Thursdays and Fridays. You can find leatherware such as sandals, jackets and bags; carpets and rugs; dresses and shirts made of cheesecloth or other handwoven materials of the region; various decorative objects such as candle-holders, ashtrays, necklaces made out of blue stone (the famous evil-eye), beads, bracelets, earrings, wooden ornaments and pottery.

USEFUL ADDRESSES
Tourism and Information Office
12 Eylül Meydanı. Tel. 10 91

Marmaris

Situated at the confluence of the Mediterranean and the Aegean, Marmaris is arguably Turkey's finest beach resort, with a beautiful, fine-sand beach and excellent hotels and restaurants. Not surprisingly, it is one of the favourite holiday haunts of Turks themselves.

The northern coast of this peninsula is the most indented of all Turkish coastlines and particularly suitable for aquatic sports.

Marmaris is now being featured extensively in holiday companies' programmes, thanks largely to the opening of Dalaman Airport, to which direct flights are now operating from many European cities. Although still 100 km. from Dalaman, Marmaris is much more accessible than hitherto.

The resort is particularly suitable for family holidays. Alongside the old fishing port is the modern yacht marina, while all along the shores of the almost landlocked bay are beaches of golden sand, with a calm sea ideal for swimming from June to late September. The resort boasts many new, modern hotels – some of international standard – and smaller pensions, as well as lots of simple restaurants in quiet coves. Lively discothèques dot the shoreline and one can hire a boat to explore the many islands in the bay – or, alternatively, join one of the organized cruises.

Marmaris, the ancient Physcus, was part of the south-west Aegean kingdom of Caria, the two most powerful cities of which were Knidos and the capital, Bodrum. Marmaris was a small trading town on the Anatolia–Rhodes–Egypt route. In the sixth century BC Caria fell to the Lydians and was then subjugated by the Persians, until Alexander the Great ousted them in 334 BC. The Romans conquered the region by 163 BC and after the division of the Roman Empire the area fell under Byzantine rule. The region was wrested from the Byzantines in AD 1282 by the Turkish Emir of Mentese, and in 1425 the rule of the Ottoman Turks was established.

Dominating Marmaris is the fortress, built by Sultan Süleyman the Magnificent in 1522 as a military base during his victorious campaign to conquer Rhodes. From the castle there is a magnificent panorama of the bay. Also dating from Süleyman the Magnificent's time are the old bridge, the Taşhan (stone inn) and the caravanserai, which is still used as an inn. Also of interest is the mosque, revealing a combination of Turkish and Arabic influence, and there is also the Evliya Sarı Ana Türbesi, the tomb of a woman who is said to have performed miracles to aid Süleyman the Magnificent.

EXCURSIONS FROM MARMARIS
Beaches around the Resort   All the following beaches are from 2–10 km. away from Marmaris by road. To the east of the resort are the beaches of **Günnücek,** surrounded by frankincense trees; **Aktaş** and **Adaköy,** with pine trees coming right down to the beach. To the west of Marmaris is a row of beaches leading up to **Gölenye Springs.** The spring water is reputed to have curative properties, especially for intestinal complaints. There are two seafood restaurants, a picnic spot and a beach nearby.

Short Boat Trips   From the harbour at Marmaris you can take a motor boat trip of the bay which will take you to the **Alkaya Caves.** There is also a tour which takes you round the bay and then on to **Turunç,** where there is a fine beach and several seafood restaurants.

Amos   It is possible to hire a boat for the fifty-minute trip to the site of ancient Amos, with its acropolis, temple and Roman theatre.

Kaunos   There are coach tours to this ancient Carian city, or, if you have a vehicle which can cover rough terrain, you can go via Köyceğiz (94 km. from Marmaris), up to which there is an asphalt road. After Köyceğiz it is necessary to take a right turning on to the earth road that leads to Kaunos. At the site one can see a theatre, baths, temples and some interesting rock tombs.

RESTAURANTS
Most of Marmaris' restaurants are situated on the sea

front. The Palmiye Restaurant and the Yarasa Tavern
have their own orchestras, and Kemal's Place is famous
for its fish. The delicious fish of the Aegean, such as red
mullet, sea bass, prawns and octopus, should not be
missed. Also in abundance is classical Turkish food,
including many varieties of kebab, pilav and stuffed
vegetables.

ENTERTAINMENT
Various seaside cafés, discothèques and open-air cinemas operate between June and September. Occasionally
there are performances of Western Anatolian folk
dances.

YACHTING, FISHING AND SKIN-DIVING
Though yachts for hire are always available in Marmaris,
it is advisable to apply to the Karia or Yeşil Marmaris
agencies to make reservations. The coasts and islands
around the resort are excellent for fishing and skin-
diving. You can fish for bream, bass and mullet, and
tunny can be caught in the neighbouring **Karaağaç Bay.**
The best places for skin-diving are **Turunç Bükü** and
Kütük Burnu. For additional information on fishing and
skin-diving it is best to consult the Tourism and Information Bureau in Marmaris.

SHOPPING IN MARMARIS
All kinds of handicrafts are available in the many small
shops around the harbour. Leather coats and jackets,
and carpets and rugs in classical oriental designs are
some of the best-quality buys. There are also many
articles in onyx, as well as embroidered blouses and other
garments.

USEFUL ADDRESSES
Information Bureau
Iskele Meydanı, No. 39. Tel. 10 35

Travel agent
Yeşil Marmaris Acentası, Kemeraltı Mah, Fevzipaşa Cad.
14. Tel. 10 33

Rent-a-car
Genco Acentası, by the harbour

Datça

From Marmaris you can make an excursion by road or
boat to Datça, a picturesque fishing village perched
above the sea on a wooden peninsula.

Fethiye

About 150 km. from Marmaris, along the coast, is
Fethiye, overlooking an attractive bay strewn with
islands. This ancient town is crowned by the ruins of a
fortress built by Knights of the Crusades, and in the steep
cliffs ancient Lycian tombs are carved out of the rock face.
Fethiye, too, has fine sandy beaches, while nearby is the
incredibly beautiful **Ölü Deniz** – a calm lagoon of crystal-
clear water, ideal for swimming and sailing.

Aphrodisias and Pamukkale

Bisecting the south-western Anatolian plateau is the fertile valley of the Meander, the Büyük Menderes. It is
from the name of this river and its serpentine lower
course that the English word meander is derived. Since
Phrygian and Carian times the region has been occupied,
successively, by the Romans, the Byzantines and the
Turks. Bordering the Meander Valley are two outstanding sites, each providing sufficient justification for a visit
to the region. Firstly, there is one of Turkey's most
beautiful archaeological sites, Aphrodisias, and,
secondly, there is the unique natural phenomenon of the
petrified waterfall of Pamukkale. Both of these sites are
easily accessible along the fine arterial road that links
Izmir and Antalya.

The ruins of Aphrodisias are located near the village of **Geyre** and form one of the most important and attractive archaeological sites in Turkey, situated as they are at the foot of the impressive Baba Dağ Mountain.

The city was the centre of the cult of Aphrodite and it possessed a flourishing school of sculpture. During the Roman period it reached the zenith of its prosperity as a religious, artistic and literary centre. Aphrodisias' huge stadium, which could accommodate 30,000 spectators, is one of the best preserved in the Roman world. Fourteen elegant columns remain standing of the Temple of Aphrodite, which was a pilgrimage centre and a place of sanctuary. Near the temple is a beautiful gateway, the propylon. There is also a small odeon or concert hall, recently excavated and miraculously undamaged, with its sunken orchestra and its stage elaborately decorated with mosaics and statuary.

Several Ionic porticos and twelve columns remain of the agora or marketplace. Also of interest are the thermal baths of Hadrian and two palatial residences that belonged to a bishop and a Byzantine official. One should not miss the fine sculptures displayed in the museum in the centre of the old village of **Geyre**. Aphrodisias is still in the process of excavation and every year new works of art are uncovered.

About 20 km. by road from the relatively new town of **Denizli** – which contains little of historic interest apart from an eleventh century Turkish bazaar within the for- tifications – is the amazing Pamukkale. The word means 'Cotton Castle' and the place is so called because the waters of thermal springs laden with calcium oxide have formed a dazzling white, petrified cascade of stalagtites 100 m. in height flowing over the plateau edge into a series of basins and pools.

On top of the plateau are the thermal baths and ruins of ancient Hierapolis. The waters of the springs have been used since Roman times. The water is just about blood heat and has a relaxing quality that is said to be good for rheumatism and arthritis. All the modern hotels on the plateau have thermal pools.

The city of Hierapolis was founded in the second century BC, but all the ruins date from the Roman period. Among the elegant buildings are the thermal baths – part of these now form a museum of sculpture. There are also the Christian Basilica, Temple of Apollo, theatre and Martyrium of Phillip, dedicated to the Apostle who was martyred here in AD 80. On the way back from the basilica to the theatre there was said to be a crack, called the Plutonion, which the ancients believed led to the Underworld. The crack was probably filled with carbon dioxide and Strabo tells how, when he threw sparrows in, they died immediately. The vast Roman and early Christian cemetery to the north of the city is one of the best preserved and most fascinating in Turkey.

Five kilometres to the north of Pamukkale are sulphurous hot-springs, the reddish-brown waters of which are said to be good for rheumatic complaints. Visitors can bathe in the pools of the hotel and camp site near the springs.

ACCESS

By Air The closest airport is that of Izmir, from which one can reach Aydın or Denizli by road or rail.

By Rail There is a daily train, the Pamukkale Mototreni, which leaves from Ankara and Istanbul for Denizli, via Eskişehir and Afyon. There are several trains a day from Izmir to Aydın (three hours) and Denizli (six hours).

By Road Aydın and Denizli lie on the international highway E24 which passes through Izmir and rejoins the coast at Antalya (Izmir–Aydın 125 km.; Izmir–Denizli 250 km.; Antalya–Denizli 290 km.). Many private coach companies have services from Izmir to Aydın and Denizli, and in the summer there are direct services from Ankara.

ACCOMMODATION
Denizli: Hotel Izmir, Hotel Koru, Hotel Sarikaya
Pamukkale: Motel Tusan and several small hotels such as
the Pamukkale, Koru, Esot, Mis-Tur and Turizm

USEFUL ADDRESSES
Tourism and Information Bureau
TCDD Gar Binası. Tel. 13 393

HOW TO GET TO THE TURKISH AEGEAN
By Air   Turkish Airlines operates direct flights from
several European capitals to Izmir, and also regular
services from Istanbul to Izmir. Dalaman Airport at
Mugla, 19 km. east of Marmaris, provides the easiest
access to the southern coastal region, although distances
are still great and transfer time quite long. However,
Dalaman is now being served by an ever-increasing
number of holiday charter flights from many European
centres.

By Boat   Turkish Maritime Lines leave Istanbul every
other Thursday for a 12-day cruise, stopping at ports on
the Aegean coast. Fares are low but the overall standards
far from luxurious. There are also frequent services to
Izmir from Marseilles and Genoa, and car-ferry links in
the summer from Venice and Brindisi.

By Train   Travelling towards the Aegean resorts by
train is not really a practical proposition for most visitors.
However, Izmir is linked by rail with Bandirma, connecting with boats from Istanbul, and there are regular
Ankara-Izmir train services.

By Road   Roads in this region of Turkey are generally
reasonably good, though often narrow and winding.
Motorists travelling from the main centres of Western
Europe can knock up to 800 km. off their journey by
using the Greek port of Piraeus and taking a car ferry
from there to the Turkish Aegean ports. However, Turkey's continuing problems with Greece sometimes result
in entry and exit problems.

The coastal road from Thrace across the Dardanelles to Bodrum, Marmaris and detouring inland via Mugla to Fethiye (mainly E24 and Route 6) is quite good; alternatively, cars can be rented easily in Izmir, and are becoming more readily available at Dalaman as demand grows.

The Mediterranean

ANTALYA — KEMER — PHASELIS — DEMRE —
SIDE — PERGE — ASPENDOS — ALANYA —
MERSIN — ADANA — ISKENDERUN —
ANTAKYA

'Among the outstanding memories which the visitor brings
away from his first visit to Antalya must surely be the view of
the Lycian mountains across the bay.'

George Bean

MARK ANTONY, it is claimed, once gave part of Turkey's
southern shore to Cleopatra as a wedding gift. If the story
is true, then the gods were certainly smiling on Cleopatra
that day, for this coast has everything befitting such a
princely gift. Set against the often snow-capped peaks of
the Taurus Mountains are the seemingly endless
stretches of white sand, lapped by the translucent waters
of the Mediterranean – which, perhaps because of its
crystalline quality, the Turks themselves call '*Ak Deniz*' or
'White Sea'. The verdant shores are covered with pine
forests, orange groves and banana plantations, splashed
here and there with the vivid pink of wild oleanders –
and mushrooming holiday complexes!

Here, legend and history are interwoven. In the mountains to the west of Antalya is the 'Chimera', the legendary fire-breathing monster that the hero Bellerophon
is said to have slain. Behind Antakya are the bay trees of

the gardens of Daphne, where the nymph was said to have been turned into a bay tree by Zeus to escape the amorous advances of Apollo. And it was from Tarsus that St Paul came, and in Demre that the original St Nicholas – a fifth-century bishop – once lived.

Like Turkey's Aegean coast, her Mediterranean coast is also littered with ancient ruins. Atop a craggy peak to the west of Antalya, like an eagle's nest, are the ruins of Termessos. On the coastal plains are the Pamphylian cities of Perge, Aspendos and Side. Perge's great stadium once seated 15,000, and the theatre of Aspendos is the best preserved in Anatolia. The ruins of Side are elegantly set on a promontory between two sandy bays.

The Antalya region – sometimes known as the Turquoise Coast or the Turkish Riviera – is one of the chief areas of extensive tourism development in Turkey and one of the most beautiful. Massive hotel construction work is taking place in an area located between the harbour of Antalya itself and the Gelidonya peninsula – a coastline of 75 km., forming part of the Bey Dağları National Park. Here, scores of hotels have either opened very recently, or will do so shortly, many with international-standard facilities.

Many more holiday hotels are also being created at the beach resort of Konyaaltı, located within Antalya city, while the harbour and ancient city quarter of Antalya has been declared an historic site and is being conserved, with the old harbour being converted into an elegant yacht marina.

This intensely colourful region is bathed in sunshine for an average of 300 days in the year and the clear turquoise waters, secluded coves, rocky headlands and broad bays fringed with sandy beaches are ideal for swimming, sailing and all water sports. It is one of the rare regions in the world where, in March and April, it is just about possible to ski in the snowy Taurus Mountains in the mornings and bathe in the Mediterranean in the afternoons.

A good asphalt road from Antalya to Antakya links the

resorts of this 500 km. coastline and the region is well connected by road to the rest of the country. In the summer Turkish Maritime Lines operates a regular service from Istanbul to Iskenderun and back, the liners calling at all the main resorts; while Turkish Airlines operates daily flights from Istanbul to Antalya. With its unspoiled natural beauty and historic sites, the 'Turkish Riviera' has an all-season appeal to both the pleasure-seeker and the lover of history. It is already a favourite holiday destination among discerning travellers.

Antalya

The principal holiday resort of the Mediterranean is the port of Antalya, situated atop the cliffs of a crescent-shaped bay surrounded by the towering peaks of the Taurus Mountains. It is an attractive, lively town with shady, palm-lined boulevards, picturesque old quarters and harbour, and a city park. There are several modern hotels in the town and it is an ideal base from which to visit the ancient sites of Lycia and Pamphylia and the shady pine woods, waterfalls and spacious beaches in the immediate vicinity. In summer Antalya hosts an annual festival featuring artists, theatre groups, folk dancing and music.

Antalya, the ancient Attaleia, was founded in the second century BC by Attalus II of Pergamon, and was conquered successively by the Romans and Seljuks. It is possible to visit all of the principal monuments either on foot or by horse-drawn carriage. There are well-preserved city ramparts and the monumental Hadrian's Gate, in beautifully decorated marble, which was built in AD 130 to commemorate the Emperor's visit to the city. Nearby is the Kesık Minare (truncated minaret), which was transformed from a Byzantine church into a mosque. At the edge of the city park, which boasts an amazing variety of exotic flowers and plants, is the Hıdırlık Kulesi, which was formerly a lighthouse. Along the road from the park to the town centre stands the Karatay Medrese (theological school), with its Seljuk-style portal.

A short distance from the town square is the identifying landmark of Antalya – the curious fluted minaret of the Yivli Minare Camii, which was converted from a church into a mosque in the thirteenth century by the Seljuk Sultan Alaeddin Keybukat and today houses a small ethnographic museum. From here one can walk downhill along the narrow winding streets of the old quarters, lined with pretty wooden houses, which lead to the harbour, where cruise ships are regular callers. On the Konyaaltı road, at the western edge of the town, is a new archaeological museum that houses a rich collection of ceramics, mosaics and figurines discovered from the surrounding areas.

EXCURSIONS AND CRUISES

The environs of Antalya offer many possibilities for short excursions, and one can join a mini-cruise to visit the ancient Lycian sites by boat. On the western edge of the town is the huge crescent of the attractive **Konyaaltı Beach** earmarked for extensive touristic development. A short distance to the east is the lovely **Lara Beach,** near to which the spectacular **Düden Waterfalls** plunge 45 m. over the cliff edge to the sea. Further up the same river are the equally spectacular **Upper Düden Waterfalls.**

The old city fortress of **Termessos** lies high in the hills to the north west of Antalya. The remains include city walls, an agora, a necropolis and a theatre perched on a sheer precipice.

Along the road to Finike is the pretty mountain town of Elmalı, on the outskirts of which is Karagöl (Black Lake), whose waters rush out into a huge chasm.

To the west of the Gulf of Antalya the Taurus Mountains of the Lycian Peninsula sweep down to the sea, and this region abounds in more or less deserted beaches and fascinating historical remains. Be warned, however: the roads are poor, although the scenic beauty of the area goes a long way towards compensating for this. Alternatively all the sites can be visited in comfort by joining one of the mini cruises that depart regularly from the harbour of Antalya.

SKIING
It is actually possible to ski in the mornings and swim in the warm Mediterranean in the afternoons at certain times of the year, providing you don't mind the water being somewhat on the cool side. The skiing resort which makes this possible is Saklıkent, situated in the Bey Dağı mountain range 48 km. north of Antalya at a height of 2,546 m. The best skiing is between January and April. The resort isn't particularly sophisticated, but accommodation is available in small hotels or pensions and family chalets.

Kemer

One of the Lycian peninsula's fastest-developing – and prettiest – holiday resorts, and one which is gaining great favour with European holidaymakers, is Kemer, located to the west of Antalya, not far from the ancient ruins of Phaselis. A luxurious new holiday village there (pictured on the cover of this book) is set in the midst of pine woods stretching right down to the sea shore.

The ruins of the ancient port of Phaselis lie on a narrow creek opening on to the Gulf of Antalya, a few kilometres south of Kemer. The city is believed to have been founded in the seventh century BC by settlers from Rhodes and it was a major port which had three harbours. Most of the remains are Roman, and a theatre (still unexcavated), an agora, a fine aqueduct, a necropolis and a Hellenistic fortress are among its attractions.

Further south is **Finike**, the ancient Phoeniscus, a lovely little resort surrounded by sandy beaches and orange groves. East of the town, off the coastal road in the Bey Dağı mountain range, is the perpetual fire which legend identifies as the 'Chimera', the fire-breathing monster. It is, in fact, burning natural gas escaping from a hole in the rock.

Demre

According to recent research, the original St Nicholas, or Father Christmas, was not born in the wintry lands of snow and igloos, but in Turkey. His actual birthplace, it is claimed, is the village of Patara, on the shores of one of the loveliest coasts of southern Turkey. And each year, on 6 December – the birthday of St Nicholas – a festival to commemorate him is held in the tiny church which carries his name in the village of Demre, to the west of Finike.

St Nicholas was Bishop of Myra in the fifth-century AD, at the time of Emperor Constantine. Legend has it that when he was young his parents died, leaving him a fortune. Nicholas used the money to help others, especially young people; he is said to have made anonymous gifts of gold to girls from families too poor to give them a dowry. As the St Nicholas cult developed over the centuries, memory of him faded in his original home town. Earlier this century the roofless basilica of St Nicholas was used as a substitute for a mosque by the people of Demre. It was only in the last decade, with the expansion of tourism, that the Turkish authorities realized the potential of the building; and after several years of restoration, the church was finally opened in 1981 as a shrine to St Nicholas. Beside the church is a statue of St Nicholas as he is known throughout the world – bearded, robed, and trundling a sackful of presents behind him.

Side

If I were asked to name a Turkish holiday resort that best combines the needs of the holidaymaker seeking a sun-sea-and-sand experience with a large slice of 'culture'

right on its doorstep, the very pretty resort of Side (pronounced See-day) would win hands down. It has a fine
location between two vast sandy beaches backing
immediately on to sand dunes and fascinating ruins,
with the Taurus Mountains forming a dramatic
backdrop.

Until comparatively recently Side was simply a small
fishing port; today, with the advent of tourism, it is fast
developing into one of Turkey's major holiday resorts,
with a wide selection of excellent hotels and good-quality
pensions to suit most tastes and budgets. The majority of
the establishments offer sea views, while adjacent to the
sea is an excellent selection of attractive and lively cafés,
restaurants and discothèques. Side's narrow streets are
lined with shops selling typical Turkish handicrafts.

The exact date of Side's foundation is not clear, but
major development took place in the seventh century BC
when it was colonized by the Greeks. It was a major Pamphylian port and most of the remaining monuments are
Roman. In the ninth and tenth centuries AD Side was
notorious for piracy and its thriving slave trade. Ruins
mark the approach to the site at quite a distance from the
resort.

The walls and towers of the ancient city are very well
preserved and the remains of an aqueduct still stand.
Opposite the entrance, outside the city walls, are an
exquisite fountain and the Roman Baths which now
house a museum displaying statues recovered from the
site. The entrance portal is flanked by two towers, while
just inside is the theatre, which dominates the site. It
could seat an audience of 20,000 and is remarkable in that
the cavea was not built on to a hill but was constructed. It
is now partially collapsed, but the covered gallery and
rows of seats are preserved. Next to the theatre is the first
agora, with porticos and shops on three sides and the
ruins of a temple dedicated to Tyche in the centre. There
is also a second agora, and scattered throughout the
remainder of the site are the ruins of temples dedicated to
Apollo and Athena; a Byzantine chapel; numerous foun-

71

tains; and the remains of private Roman houses and a harbour.

PLACES OF INTEREST NEARBY
Not far from Side, on the road to Alanya, are the **Manavgat Waterfalls**. Though not particularly spectacular, they are in a delightful setting, complete with a lovely terrace mid-stream and an attractive café.

Perge

The coast between Antalya and Alanya is intensively cultivated and indented by several streams and rivers. Here was the ancient Pamphylia, and the land bears the imprint of several civilizations. A turning from the main road at the village of Aksu leads to the ruins of Perge. Until the time of Alexander the Great Perge was an independent city republic; it then became a principal city of Pamphylia in Hellenistic times. The city prospered under Rome, its importance not declining until the Byzantine period.

Just outside the city walls is a Greco-Roman theatre which could seat an audience of 15,000. The auditorium has a colonnaded gallery running round the top and was built against a hillside. Adjacent to the theatre is an impressive stadium, one of the biggest and best-preserved of antiquity, which could seat approximately 15,000 spectators. One enters the Hellenistic enclosure through a Roman gate behind which lies a triumphal arch that has been restored by archaeologists. Further along is the handsome older city gate, dating from the third century BC, which is flanked by two lofty round towers and contains a horseshoe-shaped court. This gate leads on to a long colonnaded way that was once lined with shops and mosaic pavements. Opposite the ruins of the large agora stands a 9 m. high building which used to house the thermal baths and gymnasium.

Aspendos

A turning from the main road at Serik leads to the ruins of another important Pamphylian city, Aspendos, set on the banks of the ancient Eurymedon River. From pre-Hellenistic times the Eurymedon was navigable and Aspendos was a river port and principal city enjoying thriving commerce and trade; its local industries included the manufacture of silk and rugs. Aspendos entered into good relations with Rome after the Battle of Magnesia ad Sipylum in 190 BC and the present-day remains all date from the Roman period. Dominating the site is what is claimed to be the best preserved theatre of antiquity. Built partly against a hill, it could seat an audience of between 15,000 and 20,000. The horseshoe auditorium is divided by a gangway and surmounted by a colonnaded arcade. The acoustics are magnificent and performances of ancient Greek plays (in Turkish) are held here as part of the annual Antalya Festival.

Behind the theatre are the remains of city walls and gates, and an agora surrounded by public buildings. To the north are some of the best-preserved segments of a Roman aqueduct in Turkey. This channelled water to the city over a distance of some 32 km.

Alanya

Further along the coast is the former pirate stronghold of Alanya, which the Seljuk Sultan Alaeddin Keykubat made his winter residence. Today, Alanya is one of the Turkish Mediterranean's most important holiday resorts. The town nestles at the foot of a rocky promontory which juts out between two sandy beaches and is crowned by a Seljuk fortress. It is one of the most impressive sights to be found on the Mediterranean coast.

The town provides numerous modern hotels, motels and camping sites, while next to the sea there is a variety of fish restaurants and cafés. The road running along the sea front to the harbour is lined with innumerable boutiques selling every type of Turkish handicraft: carpets, dresses and blouses made from cheesecloth, jewellery, copper, and onyx ornaments.

The city, known in ancient times as Korakesion, was founded in the fourth century BC and, during Roman times, was a notorious pirate stronghold. The town was later annexed by Alaeddin Keykubat, who made Alanya both his winter residence and his naval base. Near the harbour are the unique arched boatyards which were built by the Seljuks, and the Kızıl Kule (Red Tower) of the same period. A new road winds its way up to the citadel and passes the picturesque cottages of the old town with their gardens full of exotic flowers and bunches of freshly dyed silk hanging out to dry.

PLACES OF INTEREST

The well-preserved double-walled fortress of Alanya has 150 towers still standing; it contains mosques, a Byzantine church, a covered bazaar, caravanserai, and cisterns. Down below is a dizzying view of the rocks fringing the promontory and contrasting with the brilliant turquoise waters of the Mediterranean; while from every side are magnificent views of the modern town, the harbour, the long beaches, and the foothills of the snow-capped Taurus Mountains.

At the foot of the promontory on the eastern side is the **Damlataş Cave,** perhaps 15,000 years old, which boasts wonderful multi-hued stalagmites and stalactites. The humidity in the cave is very high and it is claimed that a visit benefits sufferers from asthma and other respiratory complaints. Opposite the cave is a beach and nearby is the local archaeological and ethnographical museum.

Alanya is one of Turkey's major ports of entry and the harbour has been extended in recent years to accommodate a greater number of ships, including very big ones. From the harbour boats leave regularly to cruise along the surrounding shores which abound in caves and inlets. Of special interest are the **Blue Grotto,** with its phosphorescent rocks, and the **Kızlar Mağarası** (Maidens' Cave), where the pirates used to keep their female captives.

The road east of Alanya, through the village of Gazipaşa, leads to what is often claimed, and with some justification, to be the most beautiful stretch of coastline in Turkey. The road itself clings to the pine-clad mountain slopes which plunge steeply down to the sea, offering spectacular views of cliffs, coves and the brilliant turquoise waters of the Mediterranean. Just outside Anamur are the ruins of ancient **Anemorium,** with its double ramparts, a theatre, an odeon and a necropolis. The fine, well-preserved Crusader castle is nearby, set between two curving, sandy beaches, and from the top of the fort there is a splendid view of the surrounding countryside and coast.

East of Anamur the road rises and falls until one reaches the Plain of **Silifke**. Just before Silifke is the little resort of **Taşucu**, with its sandy beach and harbour from where a regular hovercraft service is operated to Cyprus. South of Silifke is **Kaya**, a Roman necropolis with the tomb and church of St Thecla, the first female martyr.

Located slightly inland is Silifke itself, set at the foot of a fortress crowning the hill that was the acropolis of the ancient Seleucia ad Calycadnos. In the town is an old bridge crossing the Calycadnos River, today called the Göksu, and the remains of a Roman theatre, temple and necropolis. To the north is **Uzuncaburç**, the ancient Olba-Diocaesarea, where architectural remains of the Hellenistic period and the impressive remains of the Temple of Zeus Olbius can be seen.

The road from Silifke to Mersin closely follows the coast, passing pines and orange groves, and is flanked on the one side by ruins of cities, basilicas and tombs, and on the other by a series of small secluded coves with sandy beaches.

Just behind Silifke at **Narlıkuyu** is a Roman mosaic depicting the Three Graces. Further on are the deep chasms known as Cennet-Cehennem (Heaven and Hell) with the ruins of a fifth-century chapel in the chasm known as Heaven. Nearby is a deep cave full of stalagmites and stalactites, believed to benefit sufferers of respiratory diseases. At the resort and ancient site of **Korykos** there is a fine sandy beach, together with modern hotels and a camp site. The Castle of Korykos stands next to the beach opposite another castle, Kız Kalesi (Maiden Castle), which stands on an islet 200 m. offshore. The two castles were once joined by a sea wall that no longer exists.

Further east are the ruins of ancient **Elaeussa**, spread over a wide area and blending in amazingly with the landscape. They include a temple, theatre, aqueducts and basilicas. Near **Kanlıdivane** are the ruins of ancient Kanytelis, with tombs resembling small temples. Viranşehir, ancient Pompeiopolis, was founded in 700 BC by the Rhodians, and among the remains are a row of Corinthian columns that once lined the Sacred Way.

Mersin

Surrounded by lush market gardens, Mersin, with its shady avenues, city park and modern hotels, is a convenient base from which to visit the nearby historical sites and numerous beaches and coves fringing the densely cultivated land. It can't really be classed as a resort. It is more a rapidly developing city and, in fact, the largest port on the Turkish Mediterranean, with a regular car ferry service to Cyprus. However, despite its very modern appearance, Mersin occupies the site of an extremely ancient city. At a large mound called Yümük Tepe, 3 km. west of Mersin, traces have been unearthed representing twelve successive settlements which date from as far back as the Neolithic period. Mersin is noted for its particularly mild winters and in this season nomadic tribes of Turcoman origin pitch their goatskin tents around the city.

PLACES OF INTEREST

To the east of Mersin, on the edge of the fertile Cukurova Plain, is **Tarsus**, the birthplace of St Paul, nestling in the foothills of the Taurus Mountains amid cedar groves. Of ancient origin, the city was conquered and invaded on several occasions, so there are few surviving remains. Relics include the Cleopatra Gate, through which Mark Antony and Cleopatra passed when they met in Tarsus; an ancient church; and the Ottoman-period Ulu Cami. Another place worth visiting is a pretty spot on the out-skirts of the town known as the **St Paul Falls,** with little streams, waterfalls and shady trees.

Adana

Set in the heart of the Çukurova Plain, on the banks of the River Seyhan, is Turkey's fourth largest city, Adana (population 700,000), the centre of a rich agricultural region and thriving cotton industry. Because of the city's long and turbulent past, there are few ancient remains. The river is spanned by the ancient Taşköprü (stone bridge), which was built by Hadrian and renovated by Justinian. Only fourteen of the bridge's original twenty-one arches are still standing. Also of interest in the city are the Akça Mescit (Chapel Mosque), the fourteenth century Ulu Cami (Great Mosque) and the ancient covered bazaar. Well worth visiting is the archaeological and ethnographical museum which houses locally exca-vated Hittite, Assyrian, Neo-Babylonian, Hellenistic and Roman remains.

PLACES OF INTEREST NEARBY

Near Adana are the **Seyhan Dam and Lake**, a pleasant spot for boating. **Karataş** is the nearest beach. Also reachable from Adana is **Misis**, which derived its wealth from its position on the caravan route between China, Persia and the Indies. There are several Roman remains to be seen, including a beautiful mosaic of the fourth century AD representing Noah's Ark and the animals. Further along the road are the ruins of the fortress Yılanlı-kale, set on the top of a rocky peak dominating the River Ceyhan.

Between Kadirli and Kozan lies the village of **Ana-varsa**, the ancient Anazarbus, where the ruins of a Roman–Byzantine city can be seen. At the neo-Hittite site of **Karatepe** are the remains of the summer residence of King Asitawada, where tablets bearing bilingual inscriptions were discovered.

Iskenderun

The road from Adana to Iskenderun crosses the Plain of Issos, where Alexander the Great defeated Darius III and the Persian Army in 333 BC. A still impressive fortress at Toprakkale, built by the Crusaders, marks the entrance to the plain. A turning from the main road just before Iskenderun leads to Yakacık, where a splendid complex of sixteenth-century Ottoman buildings, including a mosque, a covered bazaar and a fortress, make a detour here well worth while. To the north of Iskenderun is Dörtyol, formerly Issus, where one can visit the various monuments: the Cinkulesi (tower of the Jinns), a covered bazaar, a Turkish bath, a fountain and a mosque.

Iskenderun itself, formerly Alexandretta, was founded by Alexander the Great after his victory over the Persians. Today it is a busy commercial centre and port with a fine harbour. Set on the shores of a deep bay with Kızıl Dağ (Red Mountain), the ancient Mount Anamus, in the background, it is an attractive, modern city with excellent smallish hotels, restaurants and cafés along the sea front.

On the coast to the south of Iskenderun is the little fishing port of Uluçınar, lying at the foot of the Kızıl Dağ. The ruins of the ancient Antioch of Pieria are on a hill overlooking the port.

On the road to Antakya, after crossing the Belen Pass, it is possible to make a detour to the castle of Bagras, which was one of the principal strongholds of the Frankish principality of Antioch.

Antakya

Pleasantly situated in a fertile plain which extends as far as the Amik Lake, and surrounded by grand mountains, is Antakya, the ancient Antioch on the Orontes. Antakya was the prosperous and ostentatious capital of the Seleucid kings, notorious for its luxurious life and pleasures. In Roman times the city was a great centre of artistic, scientific and commercial activity. It was also a centre of Christianity; St Barnabus, St Paul and St Peter all stayed there at various times. From the end of the eleventh century, for 200 years, it was a Frankish principality held by the Crusaders.

Points of interest in the city include an old Roman bridge, a picturesque bazaar and the mosque of Habib Neccar. Of special interest is the Hatay Museum, which houses one of the richest collections of Roman mosaics in the world, all of which were discovered in the environs of Antakya. A little way beyond the town is the Grotto of St Peter, the church from which St Peter is understood to have preached for the first time and at which he founded the Christian community.

PLACES OF INTEREST NEARBY
To the south is **Harbiye**, the gardens and waterfalls of **Daphne**, city of pleasures; the **Castle of Antioch**, from which there's a magnificent view of the city, plain and sea; and the site of the ancient Seleucia of Pieria, adjacent to the vast beach of **Samandağ**.

HOW TO GET TO THE TURKISH MEDITERRANEAN
In addition to the increasing number of holiday charter flights from major European cities, Turkish Airlines operates frequent Istanbul–Antalya services, the flight

taking about one hour. THY also flies from Istanbul to
Adana (about seventy-five minutes) and from Ankara to
Adana.

By Boat   Frequent services and cruises are operated to
the principal ports on the Mediterranean coast by a
number of lines. In addition, Turkish Maritime Lines
operates summer services from Istanbul and Izmir, stopping at Fethiye, Kaş, Finike, Antalya, Alanya, Mersin
and Iskenderun. There's also a ferry boat between Mersin–Famagusta (Cyprus)–Beirut, and a hovercraft service
from Taşucu to Cyprus.

By Train   The Taurus Express operates between Istanbul–Ankara–Adana–Gaziantep–Aleppo and on to
Beirut.

By Road   Most of the Mediterranean coast is quite easily
accessible by road, especially the beautiful stretch
between Fethiye and Mersin, where the dramatic mountains rise straight from the shore.

HOTELS AND RESTAURANTS
The resorts along the Turkish Mediterranean have an
excellent selection of modern, first-class hotels and small
establishments and tiny pensions noted for their simple
comforts and warm service. Particularly impressive is the
Talya Hotel in Antalya, one of the best hotels outside
Istanbul, located on a cliff top. The hotel has 150 air-
conditioned rooms and its own heated swimming pool.
Also in Antalya, much less expensive than the Talya, is
the tiny, fifteen-room Perge Hotel, which commands
splendid views and offers swimming from the rocks. Fish
restaurants naturally abound throughout the region,
most offering well-cooked and nicely presented dishes at
remarkably low prices. Among the best known are the
Antalya Restaurant on Hastane Cad., Antalya; the Yıldız
at Adana; and Du Liban in Antakya.

USEFUL ADDRESSES

Tourism Bureaux
Antalya: Cumhuriyet Cad. No. 91. Tel. 11 747 -15 271
Alanya: Iskele Cad. No. 56. Tel. 12 40
Kemer: Belediye Binasi
Mersin: Inönü Bul. Liman Giriş Sahası. Tel.
11 265 -12 710
Antakya: Vali Ürgen Alanı No. 41. Tel. 12 636

Turkish Airlines
Antalya: Hastane Cad. Özel Idare Işhanı Altı. Tel. 12 830
Mersin: Belediye Uluçarşı 22. Tel. 15 232

Central Anatolia
ANKARA — CAPPADOCIA — KONYA

'Come, come again whoever, whatever you may be, come,
Heathen, fire-worshipper, sinner of idolatry, come,
Come, even if you broke your penitence a hundred times,
Ours is not the portal of despair or misery, come.'

Mevlâna

CENTRAL ANATOLIA, which occupies the area roughly in
the centre of Turkey, houses many of Turkey's natural
treasures, not least the amazing Cappadocia region, with
its staggering spectacles of rock cones, canyons, capped
pinnacles and underground cities. Ankara, Turkey's
capital city, is also located here, as is Konya, one of the
country's oldest continuously inhabited sites and home
of the Mevlevi sect, internationally known as the
Whirling Dervishes of Konya.

The tawny-yellow Central Anatolian plateau, slashed
by ravines and dotted with volcanic peaks, is covered
with wheat fields and lines of poplars in the valleys. The
plateau is one of the cradles of civilization, for it was here
that Çatalhöyük, thought to be the world's oldest city,
was founded in the seventh millennium BC. It has been
the homeland of many peoples and the historic
battleground of East and West. Here the Hittites and
Phrygians established their kingdoms, and in the
eleventh century the Turks made the plateau their home.

In its turbulent history the plateau has seen the march

Historic Istanbul, with boats plying the Bosphorus.

The magnificent interior of Istanbul's St Sophia museum.

The Marble Way at Ephesus, one of Turkey's most impressive historic sites.

The lovely resort of Bodrum, with its imposing Crusaders' Castle.

The beautiful lagoon of Ölü Deniz, near the holiday resort of Fethiye.

A hilltop overlooking the pretty village of Kas.

The theatre of Phaselis, to the west of Antalya.

The towers of Alanya's fascinating citadel dominate the resort.

The 'fairy chimneys' region of Cappadocia in full bloom.

The amazing clifftop monastery of Sumela, near Trabzon.

Colossal stone heads of gods on top of Mount Nemrut.

The Sat mountain range and lake, in the province of Hakkâri.

of such invaders as Alexander the Great and Tamerlane. In nine millennia, the people of the plateau have reflected in their art the dramatic contours of the surrounding landscape, from the vigorous paintings of Çatalhöyük, to the severe lines of Seljuk architecture.

Ankara

Ankara, Turkey's capital, has been built on a site chosen by the founder of the modern Turkish Republic, Mustafa Kemal Atatürk. Though the city is thoroughly modern in appearance, its origins date back to a Hittite settlement in the second millennium BC. In the eighth century BC the Phrygians established the city of Ancyra on the site, and five centuries later the Galatians made Ancyra their capital. However, it was not until after the First World War that Ankara leapt into prominence as the centre of the national resistance led by Atatürk, and on 13 October 1923 Ankara was declared the capital of the new independent Turkey. Today, Ankara is one of the most important of Turkey's industrial centres, and everywhere are smokestacks, new office buildings and other signs of its ever-increasing modernity. Yet interspersed with these is evidence of its not-forgotten past: an ancient citadel, Roman baths and Ottoman mosques.

Ankara's modern bus- and taxi-lined boulevards are sometimes interrupted by a horse-drawn carriage; ancient minarets compete with drab industrial complexes in an attempt to reach the skies; the rustic, flowing garb of village dress appears alongside contemporary fashions in modern shopping centres and old village-like bazaars.

Climatic as well as cultural differences highlight Ankara streets. The damp, mild Black Sea climate is sometimes experienced in Ankara, but nevertheless the city's winters are still cold and its summers hot and dry. Because of Turkey's topographic structure and certain external effects, the land is damp to the north of Ankara and dry to the south.

83

The province of Ankara favours cultivation, especially the raising of fruit and vegetables, and some of Turkey's choicest wines are pressed here. The region is also famous for its production of honey, wool, pears and other fruits.

VISITING THE CITY

The centre of modern Ankara is Kızılay Square, where Ziya Gökalp Caddesi and Gazi Mustafa Kemal Boulevard cross the city's major thoroughfare, Atatürk Boulevard. From Kızılay you can follow Atatürk Boulevard towards Sıhhıye. After a crossroads and a railway underpass, you will see, on the right, the buildings of Ankara University (Faculty of Literature), the Radio House and, further on, on your left, the State Opera Building and Gençlik (Youth) Park. This park, with its artificial lake, small cafés and restaurants, amusement area and other entertainments, is one of the favourite meeting places of Ankara residents. Atatürk Boulevard ends at Ulus Square, where the impressive Monument of Atatürk stands as a tribute to the War of Independence.

Head north along Çankırı Street, and 300 m. from the square you will find the Roman Baths to your left. These baths, dating from the third century BC, were built by the Emperor Caracalla and dedicated to Aesculapius, god of health. They were destroyed by fire in the tenth century, but remain fine examples of Roman architecture. The baths are famous for their column-adorned passage, vast dimensions and the impressive pathway to the gymnasium.

Returning to Ulus Square, follow the street which passes before the İş Bank until you reach Hükümet Meydanı (Government Square). Here you will find the famed Column of Julian, which stands 17 m. high and has a capitol decorated with acanthus ornaments. This column is believed to have been erected towards the end of the fourth century and is composed of fluted stones, one on top of another, rather than a single piece of rock.

Just 200 m. from Hükümet Meydanı, in the Hacı

Bayram quarter of Ulus, you can see the Temple of Augustus and the Hacı Bayram Mosque.

The Temple of Augustus was built in the second century BC in the Corinthian style. It was first dedicated to Cybele, the mother goddess of the Anatolians; then to Men, the Phrygian god of the moon; and finally to the Emperor Augustus. In the fourth century AD, after various alterations, the temple was converted into a Byzantine church, and during the Ottoman period it was called Akmedrese (the white *medrese*). As you enter the temple, on the walls to the right and left you can see a huge inscription called Testamentum Ancyranum, which describes the life and deeds of the Emperor Augustus.

The Hacı Bayram Mosque was built in the first half of the fifteenth century. It was decorated by the well-known artist Mustafa towards the end of the seventeenth century and ornamented with Kütahya tiles in the early eighteenth century.

The Tomb of Hacı Bayram Veli, after whom the mosque was named, is adjacent to the mosque. The original gate to the tomb is now in the Ethnographical Museum.

From Ulus Square the ramparts of Ankara's Citadel can be seen clearly, and a five-minute walk will take you uphill to this ancient fortress. The citadel is divided into two sections: the inner was built in the seventh century when Arab invasions were particularly frequent in Asia Minor. It dominates the top of a rocky summit and surrounds the town.

In the ninth century Mihail II had a second wall built round the first to help fortify the citadel against invasion. This outer wall surrounds the fortress in the shape of a heart. In its long history the citadel has been captured and damaged a number of times, yet twenty towers of the citadel walls are still standing. Although the actual form of these walls dates from Byzantine and Seljuk times, the building material (such as marble) came from the Romans.

Two hundred yards from the Citadel gates, near the Atpazarı (horse market), is the Museum of Anatolian Civilizations, which occupies a fifteenth-century building constructed by order of the Great Vizier Mehmet Paşa. This building once served as a *bedesten* (market of precious objects), and today it houses objects dating from the ancient palaeolithic to the classic periods. Its richest collection is that of the Hittites, and this museum is sometimes referred to as the Hittite Museum.

South-east of the citadel is Ankara's largest mosque, the Aslanhane, built by the Ahi leader Şerafettin in 1290. The interior stands on several Seljuk wooden columns; the portal is decorated with Seljuk designs; the minaret is built of brick. The altar is decorated with light-blue and black Seljuk mosaics and adorned with honeycomb stucco patterns and ornamentation in tile and brick. The pulpit (*minber*) is a fine example of walnut engraving. Adjacent to the mosque is the tomb of its patron, Şerafettin.

In the area of the citadel you can also see the small but interesting Alaeddin Mosque (twelfth century), built by the Seljuk Sultan Mesut I. Its walnut pulpit is especially noteworthy.

Not far from the Aslanhane Mosque (on Ulucanlar Street) is the sixteenth-century Mosque of Cenabi Ahmet Paşa, also called the Yeni Cami, or New Mosque. It was built by Turkey's best-known architect, Mimar Sinan and is famous for its exquisite pulpit and altar of white marble. Next to the mosque is the Tomb of Ahmet Paşa.

Coming back along Ulucanlar Street you will soon reach the Samanpazari (straw market). From here, if you follow Talat Paşa Boulevard, you will notice several original, Ottoman-style buildings (from around 1925) on your left. One of these houses the Ethnograpical Museum, which has one of the richest collections from Turkish history and folklore. Ancient dresses, carpets, ceramics, tiles, weapons, musical instruments and religious objects are among the treasures to be found here. From 1938 until 1953 the body of Atatürk rested here under a great cupola.

An alternative tour of Ankara could begin at Kızılay Square. Head south down Atatürk Boulevard and you will pass the new Parliament Building on your right, the Ankara Hotel on your left, and several embassy buildings. Continue along Atatürk Boulevard (which soon turns into Vali Reşit Boulevard) and you'll soon reach the top of Çankaya Hill, where the Presidential Palace is located. In the garden of this palace is Atatürk's House (open to the public Saturday and Sunday afternoons only), where the Founder of the Turkish Republic lived during the War of Independence and the first years of the Republic.

Head back to Kızılay Square, turn left down Gazi Mustafa Kemal Boulevard, and you will arrive at the Ministry of Tourism and Information Office where you can get pamphlets to supplement your tour. Just beyond the Ministry building is the New Maltepe Mosque and, shortly beyond that, Tandoğan Square and the grounds of Anıtkabir – the Mausoleum of Atatürk. This mausoleum, begun in 1944 and completed in 1953, stands 21 m. high and was built in the classical style. It has a porch with a monumental staircase (33 steps in all) decorated with bas reliefs. The Tower of Liberty stands to the right of this staircase; the Tower of Independence to the left. Before this stairway is an imposing paved esplanade lined with galleries and museums, its towers symbolizing the Republic, the Revolution, Victory and Peace. A magnificent alley, 30 m. wide and 260 m. long, flanked by cypress trees and twelve Hittite lions, comes to an end at the esplanade.

The mausoleum proper contains a huge inscription on its outside walls – part of a speech given by Atatürk and known as 'The Testament to Youth'. It was designed in the form of a temple surrounded by porticos with quadrangular pillars of fine travertine limestone. The walls of the main funerary chamber are faced with black and white, red-veined marble and the ceiling is sumptuously decorated with golden mosaics of purely Turkish motives. The bronze doors were made in Italy and the tomb itself is a single block of marble weighing 40 tons.

From the Mausoleum head back to Tandoğan Square, follow Çardak Street past the bus and railway stations and along Cumhuriyet (Republic) Boulevard and you will see the Hippodrome and Stadium on your left and Youth Park on your right. Just before Ulus Square you will pass the Museum of the National Assembly on your left. The first meetings of the Turkish Parliament were held in this building.

HOW TO GET TO ANKARA

Many international airlines serve Ankara's airport of Esenboğa either direct or via Istanbul, from which THY operates numerous flights a day. By train, the Istanbul–Ankara Blue Train (Mavi Tren) takes about seven and a half hours, while an alternative is the Anatolia Express night train, complete with sleeping cars. From Izmir there's an express train three times a week, which takes about twelve hours. By bus, there are regular services between Istanbul and Ankara, using the E5 Highway, about 440 km. There are excellent roads from Istanbul, Bursa (390 km.), Izmir (600 km.) and Adana (490 km.).

HOTELS AND RESTAURANTS

Ankara has a good selection of hotels at both the top end and bottom end of the market, as well as an impressive array of restaurants. Among the best hotels – and the most expensive – are the Büyük Ankara, Kent, Berlin, Dedeman, Mola and Tunalı. Hotels for those visitors on a tighter budget include the Barınak, Gül Palas, Mis, Bulduk, Efes, Paris, Akman and Alkan. Among the better-known restaurants are the RV, Gaziosmanpaşa; China Town, Gaziosmanpaşa; Washington, Bayındır Sök.; Rihtim, Rıza Şah Pehlevi Cad.; and the Liman, Kavaklıdere.

Nightlife in Ankara tends to centre on the fashionable, up-market hotels, but three recommendations are the Köşk Gazinosu and Mon Amour, Gazi Mustafa Kemal Boulevard; and the Gar Gazinosu, Istasyon Meydanı.

USEFUL ADDRESSES
Tourism Ministry
Gazi Mustafa Kemal Bul. No. 33. Tel. 29 29 30 /95

Turkish Airlines
Hipodrom Cad. Gar Yanı. Tel. 12 49 00

Turkish Touring and Automobile Club
Adakale Sok. 4/11, Yenişehir. Tel. 31 76 49

Embassies
American: Atatürk Bul. 110. Tel. 26 54 70
Australian: Nenehatun Cad. 83, Gaziosmanpaşa. Tel.
39 27 50
British: Şehit Ersan Cad. 46/A, Çankaya. Tel. 27 43 10
Canadian: Nenehatun Cad. 75 Gaziosmanpaşa. Tel.
27 58 03
Indian: Kırlangıç Sok., 24. Tel. 27 81 40 or 27 81 44
Pakistan: Iran Cad. 1. Tel. 27 23 26

Hospitals
Emergency Traffic Hospital, Balgat. Tel. 23 03 08
Ankara Hospital, Plevne Cad. Tel. 19 21 80

PLACES OF INTEREST NEARBY
Ankara's immediate environs offer a number of quiet
'getaways', ideal for brief outings or excursions.

Atatürk Orman Çiftliği (Atatürk Farm)   Located 5 km.
west of Ankara, the farm grounds contain several parks,
restaurants and a zoo.

Çubuk Barajı (Çubuk Dam)   This is 10 km. north of the
city. Here you will find undulating terrain, forest-
covered slopes and a tranquil lake.

Bayındır Barajı (Bayındır Dam)   This is 15 km. east of
Ankara, just off the Ankara–Çorum highway, with a
modern swimming pool, good restaurants and cafés.
There's an excellent camping site near the dam.

Cappodocia

It's little wonder that the ancient Roman province of Cappadocia is fast becoming a major tourist attraction in its own right, for it is a region of uniquely spectacular geomorphology. Erosion of the soft rock has resulted in a strange and magical world of pillars, cones and 'fairy chimneys', like a lunar landscape.

Tours of Cappadocia are now being featured by a growing number of international travel companies, sometimes involving a stop for a night or two in one of the new hotels built to satisfy the tourist invasion. The main tourist accommodation centres of Cappadocia are Ürgüp and Nevşehir.

The climate of the region is dry and sunny in both summer and winter, but the best times for visiting are the spring and autumn. However, even in the hottest months of July and August the heat is never excessive and the nights are always cool.

ÜRGÜP

About 23 km. east of the town of Nevşehir, Ürgüp is at the foot of a cliff riddled with troglodyte dwellings in the giant cones and chimneys, many of which are still inhabited. Since ancient times men have hollowed out troglodyte dwellings in the soft rock and here, in the dawn of Christianity, the early Christians constructed churches and monasteries and even underground cities where they could shelter from their persecutors. In addition to several hotels and pensions, Ürgüp is also a good place to buy locally made woven rugs and carpets. About 44 km. south of Ürgüp are the amazing underground cities of Kaymaklı and Derinkuyu, where level upon level of intricately planned living accommodation, palaces and chapels descend to 120 m. below the surface, complete with ventilation shafts and water supplies.

NEVŞEHIR

Nevşehir, the ancient Nissa, is a city of square stone houses typical of the region. The city developed greatly in the eighteenth century under the Grand Vizier Ibrahim Pasha, who came from Nevşehir. Dating from this period is the Kurşunlu Mosque, built by Ibrahim Pasha, and from the Seljuk period there is the Kaya Mosque.

GÖREME

Lying 18 km. north-west of Ürgüp, this monastic complex of rock chapels covered with frescoes is one of the best-known sites in Central Anatolia and an absolute tourist 'must'. Most of the chapels date from the tenth and eleventh centuries of the Byzantine period and many of them are built on an inscribed cross plan, with a central cupola supported by four columns.

In several churches are rock-cut tombs. Some of the most famous of the Göreme churches are the Elmali Kilise (Church with an Apple), the smallest and most recent of the group; the Karanlık Kilise (Dark Church), with its fine paintings and attached refectory where a long table and benches have been carved from the rock; the Çarıklı Kilise (Church with Sandals), named after the two footprints under the fresco of the Ascension; and the Yılanlı Kilise (Church with Snakes), which has fascinating frescoes of the damned in the coils of serpents.

A short way from the main Göreme group, on the road to Avcılar, is the Tokalı Kilise (Church with a Buckle), decorated with very fine tenth-century New Testament scenes. Scattered round the Göreme complex are many interesting but less accessible churches, such as the El Nazar Kilisesi, the Kılıçlar Kilisesi and the Saklı Kilise. On the road leading north from Göreme are the troglodyte village of Avcılar, with its houses attached to rock cones; Çavuşin, with its churches in a rock face; the red-coned monastic complex of Zelve; and finally Avanos, a village famous for its pottery and onyx.

On the road from Avanos back to Nevşehir is the village of Uçhisar, clustered round a rock pinnacle, from which there is a spectacular view of the whole erosion basin. Off the Nevşehir–Ürgüp road is Ortahisar, another village at the foot of a crag honeycombed with caves.

Soğanlı is located 73 km. south-west of Nevşehir. It is a valley containing about sixty chapels, some of which have had the natural rock cones above them carved into domes.

Kaymaklı and **Derinkuyu** (21 and 37 km. south of Nevşehir) are intriguing underground cities of rooms interconnected by tunnels. They were used in Byzantine times as refuges from Arab raids.

Hacıbektaş (43 km. north of Nevşehir) is a town with a beautifully preserved seminary of the Bektaşi order of dervishes and the *türbe* (mausoleum) of the order's founder, the thirteenth-century mystic Bektaş Veli.

NİĞDE

The 'Nahita' of Hittite times, Niğde is situated 342 km. from Ankara in a valley flanked by volcanic peaks, commanding an ancient trade route from Anatolia to the Mediterranean. Niğde's castle owes its present form to the Seljuks, and from the same period is the elegant Alaeddin Mosque. Dating from the fourteenth-century period of Mongol rule are the Sungur Bey Mosque and Hüdavent Hatun Türbesi, one of the finest mausoleums of Anatolia. The fifteenth-century Ak Medrese is now a museum.

Eski Gümüş is 9 km along the Niğde–Kayseri road. The Byzantine monastery and church with their fresco-covered walls date from the tenth and eleventh centuries.

Bor was a former Hittite settlement and its historic buildings include the Seljuk Alaeddin Mosque and an

Ottoman covered bazaar. It is located 14 km south of Niğde.

Kemerhisar was the site of the important Hittite city Tyana. It is 5 km south of Bor.

Aksaray was an important town in Seljuk times, although most of its historic buildings date from the fifteenth century, such as the Ulu Cami and the Zinciriye Medresesi. Aksaray is 109 km north-west of Niğde.

Ihlara is 15 km from Aksaray on the Nevşehir road. Here the Melendiz River has eroded an impressive canyon, into which Byzantine rock chapels with frescoes have been cut. A visit is best accompanied by a guide in order to appreciate fully the twenty or so churches, some of the best known of which are the Sümbüllü Kilise (Church with Hyacinths) and the Direkli Kilise (Columned Church).

KAYSERI

Kayseri, the Roman Caesarea and capital of the province of Cappadocia, lies at the foot of the extinct volcano Erciyes Daği. Close to the Byzantine fortress is the Huand Mosque and Medrese and the Mahperi Hatun Türbesi, a complex erected in the thirteenth century by the wife of Sultan Alaeddin Keykubat, the Princess Mahperi. Further to the south of the complex is the beautifully decorated Döner Kümbet of 1276, the Archaeological Museum and Köşk Medrese, a Mongol building of classical simplicity. Close to the city's covered bazaar is the much restored Ulu Cami (Great Mosque), originally built in the twelfth-century. Of Kayseri's many *medreses*, the Çifte Medrese is the most interesting, since it was the first medieval medical school of Anatolia.

Kültepe is 21 km. beyond the village of Kayseri, on the Sivas road. This was the site of the Hittite city of Makesh, though only the foundations can now be seen. Many finds from this site are on display in Kayseri's Archaeological Museum.

Sultan Han is a caravanserai built by Sultan Alaeddin Keykubat in the early thirteenth century and is one of the most beautiful in Anatolia. It is located 46 km beyond Kayseri on the Sivas road.

KIRŞEHIR
Founded in ancient times, Kırşehir became in the Middle Ages the centre of the Ahi Brotherhood, a Moslem sect based on moral and social ideals that played an important role in the spiritual and political life of Anatolian towns. Among Kırşehir's many fine Seljuk buildings are the Caca Bey Mosque of 1272 (a former astronomical observatory), the Alaeddin Mosque of 1230 and the Ahi Evran Mosque; next to the latter is the *türbe* (mausoleum) of the founder of the Ahi sect.

ESKİŞEHIR
Known in classical times as Dorylaion, Eskişehir was founded in the first millennium BC by the Phrygians. Flowing through the city is the river Porsuk, and the thirteenth-century Alaeddin Mosque and the sixteenth-century Kurşuhlu Mosque are both interesting places to visit.

PHRYGIAN SITES
Gordion was the Phrygian capital. Here Alexander the Great cut the Gordion Knot that gave him the key to Asia. At the site is the great earth tumulus of King Midas, famed for his 'golden touch'. The foundations of the ancient city can still be seen.

Pessinus was the Phrygian cult centre. Among the ruins is the Temple of Cybele, the mother goddess.

Midas Şehri 115 km. south of Eskişehir is the rock-cut cult monument of Yazılıkaya, inscriptions and rock tombs.

Çankırı was called Gangrea in the third century and Kangri until Ottoman times. Above the city are the ruins of an eleventh-century fortress, and within the city is the Ulu Cami (Great Mosque), built by Turkey's famed architect Sinan in the sixteenth century. Just outside the city is the Taş Mescit of 1235, a medieval hospital.

Çorum was known as Nikonia in Byzantine times. The city adopted its present name after the eleventh-century Turkish conquest. Of interest is the thirteenth-century Ulu Cami (Great Mosque) and the nineteenth-century clock-tower.

HITTITE SITES
The Hittites were a proud and war-like Indo-European people who ruled Anatolia from 2000 to 1180 BC. All the Hittite sites now lie in Çorum province.

Boğazkale the Hittite capital of Hattusas, is ringed with double walls, broken by the Royal Gate, the Lion Gate and the Yer Kapı (an underground tunnel). The largest ruins on the site are those of the Great Temple of the storm god of Hattusas, surrounded by seventy store rooms. In 1180 BC Hattusas was devastated by the Phrygians. Just outside the village of Boğazköy is a small Archaeological Museum which is worth a visit.

Yazılıkaya is an open-air rock sanctuary containing fine reliefs of Hittite gods and kings dating from the thirteenth century BC.

Alacahöyük was the centre of a flourishing Hattian Bronze Age culture, before the arrival of the Hittites, and it was from the Royal Tombs of this period that the magnificent gold and bronze objects in Ankara's Museum of Anatolian Civilizations were uncovered. All the standing remains, such as the Sphinx Gate, date from Hittite times.

Yozgat is the newest of all the cities of Central Anatolia, being founded in the eighteenth century under the Ottomans. Dating from this period is the Çapanoğlu Mosque and the adjacent Süleyman Bey Mosque.

AMASYA

Set in a narrow gorge of the Yeşilırmak, Amasya, the ancient Amaseia, was, from the third to the second century BC the capital of the Pontic Kingdom, and it was the birthplace of the ancient geographer Strabo. On the craggy rock face of the gorge are the ruins of the citadel, inside which are the remains of an Ottoman palace and a secret underground passageway. Hewn from the rock face above the town are the impressive rock tombs of the Pontic kings. Among the city's many historic buildings are the Fethiye Mosque, once a seventh-century Byzantine church; the thirteenth-century Seljuk Burmalı Minare Mosque; the Toruntay Türbesi; and the Gök Medrese, now a museum housing the interesting mummies of the Mongol Ilhanid rulers of Amasya.

Merzifon is 50 km. north-west of Amasya. Of interest in the town are several Ottoman monuments such as the Celebi Sultan Mehmet Medresesi and the Kara Mustafa Paşa Mosque.

Borabay Lake is 60 km. north-west of Amasya. This beautiful crater lake is set amid forests in spectacular mountain scenery.

TOKAT

At a distance of 422 km. from Ankara, the ancient settlement of Comana Pontica was situated some 8 km. from the present site of Tokat, and it was only after the eleventh-century Turkish conquest that the settlement grew up here. Among the city's many historic buildings are the ruins of the 28-tower castle; the twelfth-century Garipler Mosque; the sixteenth-century Ali Pasha Mosque; and the seventeenth-century Ulu Cami. The

Pervane Bay Darüşşifası (or Gök Medrese), one of Tokat's finest buildings, is now a museum. Spanning the Yeşilirmak is a twelfth-century Seljuk bridge.

Niksar (69 km. north-east of Tokat) is at the site of the Roman Neo Caesarea and one time capital of the Turkish Danişmend Emirs. There is a well-preserved citadel, as well as the twelfth-century Yağibasan Medresesi and the Ulu Cami.

Zile is 70 km. west of Tokat. It was here that Julius Caesar pronounced the famous words, *'Veni, vidi, vici'* (I came, I saw, I conquered). Beneath the fortress is the restored Ulu Cami of 1269.

SIVAS

Known as Sebasteia under the Romans, Sivas was an important commercial centre on the crossroads of the Persia and Baghdad caravan routes. From AD 1142 to 1171 it was the capital of the Turkish Danişmend Emirs. In 1919 the Turkish National Congress was held in Sivas. Historic buildings here include the Danişmend Ulu Cami, thirteenth-century Şifaiye Medresesi and the beautifully decorated Gök Medrese, Çifte Minare Medrese and Buruciye Medresesi, all dating from 1271.

HOW TO GET TO CAPPADOCIA

By Air   There are direct flights from many European capitals to Ankara's international airport of Esenboğa, and numerous flights a day from Istanbul's airport, Yeşilköy. From Istanbul and Ankara there are several flights a week to Kayseri.

By Rail   Between Istanbul and Ankara there are daily day and night express services (see 'Ankara' section), and between Ankara and Kayseri there is also a daily express service. A daily motor train service operates from Istanbul to Konya.

By Road   There are frequent and cheap coach services operated by private companies between Istanbul and Ankara, and from Ankara to all the major centres of the region. Several car rental agencies operate in Ankara.

HOTELS
Small hotels are scattered throughout Cappadocia, but most visitors tend to stay in the Ürgüp and Nevşehir areas, where there are several new hotel developments. The following establishments have official tourist licences.

Nevşehir
Orsan Kapadokya, Kayseri Cad. Tel. 1035 2115 2554
Göreme, Hükümet Cad. 16. Tel. 706
Lale, Belediye Yanı. Tel. 1797 2995

Ürgüp
Büyük. Tel. 60 61
Sinasos, Mustafapaşa. Tel. 09
Tepe. Tel. 74
Turban Ürgüp (one of the best). Tel. 490

USEFUL ADDRESSES
Tourism Bureaux
Kayseri: Kağnı Pazarı 61. Tel. 11190 19295
Kırşehir: Aşık Paşa Cad. Cumhuriyet Mey. Tel. 1416
Nevşehir: Lale Cad. 20/A. Tel. 1137
Niğde: Istiklal Cad. Vakıf Işhanı 1/D. Tel. 261
Sivas: Hükümet Binası. Tel. 3535 2850
Ürgüp: Kayseri Cad. 37. Tel. 159

Turkish Airlines
Kayseri: Sahabiye Mah. Yıldırım Cad. 1. Tel. 13 947

Camping Sites
Kervansaray Göreme Mocamp, on the Nevşehir–Ürgüp road, 2 km. from Nevşehir
Koru Mocamp. Tel. 2776
Paris Camp, on the Nevşehir–Ürgüp Road, 6 km. from Ürgüp

Konya

In the heart of the Anatolian plateau, 260 km. south of Ankara, lies the holy city of Konya, famous for its beautiful Seljuk architecture and for its connection with the great mystic poet Mevlana, founder of the sect now known throughout the world as the Whirling Dervishes of Konya.

The Plain of Konya fans out from the foothills of the Taurus Mountains. Here, on the grasslands in Neolithic times, the wild bull and leopard roamed. These animals became the cult figures of Çatal Höyük, thought to be the world's first city.

Konya itself is a very ancient city; indeed, according to Phrygian legend, it was the first city to emerge after the Flood. There was a prehistoric and later a Hittite settlement here, but the first important town was founded by the Phrygians, who were succeeded by Lydians, Persians and the Seleucid kings of Pergamon. In Roman times it was already an important centre of trade. St Paul and St Barnabas both visited Konya on several occasions.

It was in the twelfth century that the Konya Plain experienced its second cultural renaissance when the city became the capital of the Seljuk Turks. Migrating from the steppes of Central Asia, the Seljuks served the Byzantines a crushing defeat in 1071 at Malazgirt, which opened the floodgates to the Turkish settlement of Anatolia. Under the enlightened rule of the Sultan Alaeddin Keykubat, Seljuk culture reached its zenith in thirteenth-century Konya. It was in this environment that one of the great Moslem mystic movements was born.

Celaleddin Rumi, known as Mevlana, was born in Belh, Khorassan, in 1207, the son of an eminent theologian. When Genghis Khan's Mongol hordes attacked Belh, the family fled westwards, and after many wanderings they came to Konya at the invitation of the Sultan. On the advice of his spiritual guide, Burhaneddin, Mevlana travelled to Aleppo and Damascus, where he met the greatest philosophers of the time, before returning to Konya, where he began teaching his disciples.

Mevlana's tolerance and humanity were quite exceptional for his age and the period during which he lived. As the symbol of the shedding of earthly ties, he devised the whirling dance, accompanied by the ethereal sound of the reed flute. This whirling dance can still be seen each December, during the annual Mevlana Festival.

Not surprisingly, the most famous building in Konya is the Mevlana Mausoleum, the old monastery where the Order of Dervishes was founded. Dominated by a conical, turquoise-blue dome, the complex today houses a remarkable museum of Islamic art (open every day except Mondays). Of special interest are the earliest manuscript of Mevlana's great mystic epic poem, the Mesnevi, and some of the few surviving illuminated manuscripts, as well as early musical instruments, dervish garments and fine prayer rugs.

Near to the mausoleum is the Alaeddin Mosque, completed during the reign of Alaeddin Keykubat. The wooden roofing is supported by forty-two Roman columns, and the *mimber* (pulpit) and *mihrab* (altar) are masterpieces of wood-carving.

Opposite the mosque is the Karatay Medresesi, which was built in the thirteenth century and has a beautiful marble portal. It now houses the Museum of Ceramics (open every day except Monday), with beautiful displays of rare Seljuk ceramics.

Beside the Alaeddin Park is the Ince Minareli Medrese, its splendid portal decorated with intricate natural motifs. The building is now a museum of stone and wood carvings, including many fine Seljuk pieces. The Archaeological Museum displays many fine Greco-Roman pieces from ancient Iconium.

The lively bazaar is a good place to buy carpets, especially famous in Konya for their beautiful colours and fine quality.

PLACES OF INTEREST NEARBY

Sille lies 10 km. north of Konya. A Byzantine church and several rock chapels with frescoes can be visited.

Çatalhöyük, which is 35 km. south of Konya, is a fascinating Neolithic site dating back to the seventh millennium BC. It is one of the world's oldest towns where the mud houses were entered by holes in their roofs. The famous bull and mother goddess cult figures from the site are now displayed in Ankara's Archaeological Museum.

Karaman, 110 km. south of Konya, was formerly the capital of the medieval Karamanid Emirate, the first Turkish state to use Turkish as the official language rather than Persian. Also in the town is the burial place of Yunus Emre, the first great poet to write in Turkish in the thirteenth century. The castle dates from Seljuk times, and among the many beautiful Karamanid buildings are the Araboğlu, Yunus Emre and Aktekke Mosques, and the Hatuniye Medresesi.

Alahan lies 50 km south of Karaman. Here are the quite well-preserved remains of a Byzantine monastery and a Seljuk caravanserai.

Ivriz is the site of one of Turkey s finest neo-Hittite reliefs of a king and fertility god.

Beyşehir, 92 km. west of Konya, is set on the banks of Turkey's third largest lake. Of interest are the beautiful Seljuk Eşrefoğlu Mosque and Medrese.

Eflatun Pınar has an unusual Hittite rock relief, set beside the lake.

Akşehir is famous as the birthplace of the thirteenth-century Turkish humorist Nasrettin Hoca, whose mausoleum can be seen in the town. Also of interest are the thirteenth-century Great Mosque and the Altınkale Mescidi. The Sahip Ata Türbesi is now a museum.

USEFUL ADDRESSES
Tourism Bureaux
Mevlana Cad. No. 21. Tel. 11074 20926

Turkish Airlines
Mevlana Cad. 39. Tel. 12032

The Black Sea
KILYOS – ŞILE – AKÇAKOCA – EREĞLI –
ZONGULDAK – AMASRA – BARTIN – BOLU –
KASTAMONU – SINOP – BAFRA – ÜNYE –
ORDU – GIRESUN – TRABZON – MONASTERY
OF SUMELA – GÜMÜŞHANE – RIZE – HOPA –
ARTVIN

Now we were among the rhododendrons and the azaleas
which had supplied the madding honey to the Ten Thousand
. . . and I thought the Garden of Eden had possibly been
situated here.'

Rose Macaulay

TURKEY'S BLACK Sea coast hasn't really been opened up to
international tourism yet, though it seems only a matter
of time before it will be. There are already established
resorts catering to Turkish holidaymakers – and the more
adventurous international travellers – complete with
reasonable quality, though usually unsophisticated, if
not basic, hotels and restaurants. But because the sea
tends to be considerably colder than either the Aegean or
the Mediterranean, and the sand less fine, Turkish
authorities, and travel firms, see the latter two regions as
being the ones most tourists are likely to seek out; and
they are being developed accordingly, at the Black Sea
coast's expense.

As a result, road surfaces are not always good, and in some cases pretty hopeless. There is not as yet, for example, a good road along the western coast of the Black Sea, but the ports and resorts are accessible via the interior roads. The best way to visit the area, however, is by boat, and Turkish Maritime Lines operates a weekly service between Istanbul and Hopa, calling in at all the main resorts. There are also direct flights from Ankara and Istanbul to Samsun and Trabzon.

With their densely forested mountains giving way to tea terraces, hazel-nut groves and tobacco plantations, the Black Sea shores of Turkey are exceedingly attractive . . . certainly not the arid desert that one somehow imagines. The rugged Black Sea mountains plunge steeply towards the sea, making this coastline one of craggy cliffs and headlands interrupted by sandy beaches. And, because of the mountainous nature of the region, much of the settlement is scattered over hill slopes, with the only agglomerated settlements being the towns and fishing villages of the narrow coastal belt.

Cut off from the rest of Turkey by the Black Sea chain, the Black Sea coast has pursued a somewhat independent history. According to legend these shores were the land of the Amazons, and an Amazon queen is said to have founded Sinop. In the latter Middle Ages the coast once again became the centre of an independent empire, the Comnene Empire of Trebizond (now Trabzon).

Trebizond was the last Byzantine city to hold out against the Ottoman Turks, and it was only eight years after the fall of Constantinople (Istanbul) that the last Comnene emperor surrendered to Sultan Mehmet II the Conqueror. From this rich past, fascinating remains can be seen on all sides.

THE WESTERN BLACK SEA COAST

Along the western part of the Black Sea coast are several small resorts with sandy beaches – but not always as fine sand as at some of the Aegean and Mediterranean resorts.

Kilyos

This is a delightful holiday spot in which to relax, with a good beach, comfortable small hotels and motels, and camping sites.

Şile

Located 80 km. north-east of Istanbul, Şile is a pleasant seaside resort with an attractive beach, set at the foot of jagged rocks and cliffs and dominated by the tower of a Genoese castle. The famous 'Şile bezi', the cheese cloth with which embroidered blouses and summer dresses are made, originates from here.

Akçakoca

A resort with a large sandy beach and a few small guest houses. Nearby are the ruins of a Genoese fortress.

Ereğli

Situated 40 km. to the east of Akçakoca, Ereğli is perched on a hill by the site of a ruined Byzantine citadel. In the surrounding area are various caves from one of which legend has it that Hercules descended into the underworld.

Zonguldak

A major city and a centre of coal production, Zonguldak is situated 65 km. east of Ereğli. But while the town itself is of little interest to the holidaymaker, it is close to a small town which is attracting ever-increasing numbers of international visitors: **Safranbolu.** It is here that one finds some of the most beautiful and most-admired examples of Turkish wooden houses, the majority of which have been painstakingly restored.

Amasra

A charming seaside resort lying on a peninsula cut by two creeks, and occupying the heart of a mountainous bay, Amasra is rightly considered one of the most attractive sites of the Black Sea coast. On the rocky peak of the peninsula stands the ramparts of the Byzantine citadel. There is also a Byzantine church, now called the Fatih Camii, and a Roman necropolis.

Bartın

Located 17 km. south-east of Amasra is the pretty village of Bartın, noted for its attractive timbered houses. Also of interest are the remains of a Roman road dating from the time of the Emperor Claudius.

Inebolu

From Amasra to Sinop the road is poor, but passes through beautiful scenery of forested mountains descending to the sea. Inebolu lies on this road, and is also served by Turkish Maritime Lines ships. There are some lovely beaches in the surrounding areas, notably that of **Abana.**

Bolu

Inland, in the west of the region, is an important centre on the Ankara–Istanbul road. In the city, known as Claudiopolis in Roman times, is a fourteenth-century Ulu

Camii, while 55 km. south-west is Lake Abant, situated in lovely surroundings at an altitude of 1,500 m. At **Kartalkaya**, in the Köroğlu mountains, there is a small ski centre.

Kastamonu

Located amidst forests, Kastamonu boasts a twelfth-century Byzantine church at the foot of a hill. The spectacularly carved wooden door taken from the Ibni Neccar Camii is protected in the town museum, and one should also see the thirteenth-century Atabey Camii. Near the town is Ev Kaya, a rock-tomb dating from the sixth century BC. In the nearby village of Kasaba is one of the loveliest mosques in Turkey, the Mahmut Bey Camii, while on the Kastamonu–Çankırı road in the Ilgaz Mountains is a state park and ski resort.

EASTERN BLACK SEA COASTS

Sinop

Located 462 km. north-east of Ankara is Sinop, one of the best natural harbours of the Black Sea. It was the birthplace of the Cynic philosopher Diogenes, and of Mithradates VII (135 BC), King of Pontus, and from this period date the town citadel and the foundations of a temple dedicated to Serapis. The thirteenth-century Alaeddin Camii and the Alaiye Medrese should also be seen. In the immediate area are several little fishing spots with attractive restaurants and cafés. Also close by is the picturesque village of **Gerze**, with its pleasant beach, fish restaurants and park.

Bafra

A town famous for its tobacco, caviar and thermal springs, Bafra is located 120 km. east of Sinop. Of interest are the thirteenth-century baths (hamam) and a fifteenth-century mosque-mausoleum-medrese complex.

Samsun

Located 417 km. from Ankara, Samsun is a modern industrial town and the Black Sea's most important port. It is from here that the agricultural products of the region are exported, and it is also the setting of a large fair held every July. The equestrian statue of Atatürk in the town is a reminder that Atatürk landed here in May 1919, to organize the resistance of the Turks against the partitioning of the country. Among the mosques of the town, the fourteenth-century Pazar Camii and Büyük Cami of the last century, are the most interesting.

Ünye

At a distance of 89 km. east of Samsun, Ünye is a pretty port where the purple of the rocks contrasts with the blue of the sky and the green of the hazel-nut plantations. There is a magnificent eighteenth-century hotel in the town, while 3 km. beyond the port is the lovely beach of **Çamlık.**

Ordu

Located 75 km. east of Ünye, and known in ancient times as Cotyora, Ordu stands at the foot of a verdant hill, and it was from here that the survivors of Xenophon's Ten Thousand embarked. Specially remarkable are an eighteenth-century church and the beach of **Güzelyalı**, 2 km. from the town.

Giresun

Giresun was founded by the ruins of a Byzantine fortress, and from here the Roman general and gourmet Lucullus carried the first cherry trees to Europe and transplanted them. In the town there is an eighteenth-century church, while just outside is Giresun Adası (Giresun Island), which is said to have belonged to the legendary Amazons. The island contains remains of a temple which, according to Herodotus, was dedicated by the Amazons to the god Mars. Between Giresun and Trabzon, surrounded by wooded mountains, are the villages of **Keşan, Tirebolu** – with its Byzantine–Genoese Fortress – **Vakfikebir**, and **Akçaabat**, with its old church of St Michael.

Trabzon

Situated 345 km. to the east of Samsun, Trabzon, the Byzantine Trebizond, is set against a background of wooded hills. The town is shaped like an amphitheatre next to the sea, and was founded in the seventh century BC by Miletian colonists. Later, Alexis Comnenos founded the Comnene Empire here, and this lasted until 1461. Later still, the city fell into the hands of the Ottomans.

On entering the city, on a green hill descending to the sea, is a well-preserved Byzantine monument: the thirteenth-century Aya Sofya church, the walls of which are decorated with some of the finest examples of Byzantine frescoes to be found anywhere. Inside the old citadel is the Fatih Camii, an old Byzantine church with a dome magnificently constructed in square stones, and panels of mosaics. Other interesting sights include the Ottoman mosque, Gülbahar Hatun Camii, and the old section of the upper town, which has well-preserved ramparts and a network of narrow streets lined with wooden houses. A house in which Atatürk once stayed has been turned into a museum.

After Trabzon the land of tea terraces begins, while covering the uncultivated slopes are purple wild rhododendrons, another plant that originated in this fertile region.

The Monastery of Sumela

Located 54 km. from Trabzon, and set like a swallow's nest on a sheer rock face, is the incredible Monastery of Sumela, a fourteenth-century edifice dedicated to the Virgin Mary. Alexis Comnene III was crowned here in 1340, and it is the most important Byzantine work of the region, a maze of passages, paths and chapels containing fourteenth- and fifteenth-century frescoes. If you see nothing else of Turkey's Eastern Black Sea coast, don't miss the Monastery of Sumela!

Gümüşhane

Founded on the slopes of the Zigana Mountains, and standing on the main route from Trabzon to Iran, Gümüşhane was once of considerable importance. Of interest today are historic mosques and bath-houses, and architecturally interesting houses, churches and tombs.

Rize

Located 76 km. from Trabzon, Rize is a typical Black Sea town with the natural, scenic beauty of the region. Built upon the mountain slopes along the sea-shore, the town is surrounded by tea plantations that provide its economic wealth. Of interest are the sixteenth-century Islam Paşa Camii and the remains of a Genoese fortress.

Turning inland after Ardeşen, on the road leading east from Rize, one comes to the attractive little village of **Çamlıhemşin.**

Hopa

On forested, mountain slopes 113 km. to the east of Rize, Hopa is the last port before the Turco–Russian border. Many rhododendrons grow on the summits of the mountains, while the road between Hopa and Artvin follows the spectacular gorges of the Çoruh Nehri.

Artvin

Located 62 km. south-east of Hopa, Artvin is the principal town of the province and stands at the foot of a hill crowned by the ruins of a sixteenth-century castle.

HOW TO GET TO THE BLACK SEA
Turkish Airlines operates flights from Istanbul and Ankara to Samsun and Trabzon.
By Train   From Istanbul you can take the Eastern Express to Erzurum and Kars, and then a bus to the coast.

By Bus   There are connections to all the provincial centres.

By Boat   In the summer, Turkish Maritime Lines operates an Istanbul–Hopa service, a nine-day round trip on rather basic but inexpensive 'floating hotels'.

By Road   Şile is linked with Istanbul by Route 25, a largely coastal road. The Ankara–Çorum road passes through the mountainous North Anatolian range.

HOTELS AND RESTAURANTS
On the whole, hotels on the Black Sea coast have not

reached the standards of those on Turkey's Aegean and
Mediterranean shores, but nevertheless there are
numerous small, unpretentious establishments noted for
their warm hospitality and simple but wholesome
cuisine.

There are many good restaurants in all the small towns
and villages along the coast, the better-known ones
including the Idris, Belediye and Sarayı Alti, at Bolu; the
Varan Turizm between Düzce and Bolu; and the Belediye
Sahil, Sahil Yolu, Trabzon.

Specialities of the region include many different kinds
of fish, notably turbot (*kalkan*), tunny (*palamut*), red
mullet (*barbunya*), bluefish (*lüfer*), mullet (*kefal*), and
anchovy (*hamsi*), the most plentiful fish of the Black Sea
which forms the staple diet in all the fishing villages
along the coast.

SHOPPING

The beautiful carpets of Ladik are among the best in
Anatolia, and can be bought in Samsun. Trabzon is noted
for its coin-work (finely crafted into jewellery) and for
copper objects; Rize for its tea – although the best teas are
destined for export – and for the delicate fabric known as
'Rize bezi'.

USEFUL ADDRESSES
Tourism Bureaux
Samsun: Irmak Cad. Özel Idare Işhanı A Blok, No. 2. Tel.
11 228
Trabzon: Taksim Cad. No. 31. Tel. 12 722 – 13 827
Ordu: Sahil Cad. Belediye Bınası. Tel. 1 41 78

Turkish Airlines
Samsun: Kazımpaşa Cad. 11/A. Tel. 18 260
Trabzon: Kemerkaya Mah Meydan Parki Karşısı. Tel.
13 446
Rize: Belediye Karşısı. Tel. 11 007

Turkish Touring Club
Trabzon: Iskender Paşa Mah. Meydan Camii Sok, 17/11.
Tel. 17 156

Camp Sites
Şile: Kumbaba Camping, 55 km. from the Bosphorus
Bridge. Akkaya Camping, 70 km. from the Bridge.
Akçakoca: Esentepe Camping, 3km. to the west of the
town.
Trabzon: Uzunkum Camping, 3 km. to the west of the
town.

Eastern Turkey

ERZINCAN — ERZURUM — KARS — AĞRI — DOĞUBAYAZIT — MALATYA — ELAZIĞ — TUNCELI — BINGÖL — MUŞ — BITLIS — ESKI AHLAT — AKDAMAR — VAN — HAKKARI — KAHRAMAN MARAŞ — NEMRUT DAĞI — GAZIANTEP — URFA — HARRAN — DIYARBAKIR — MARDIN

'The day of my birth will be a day of feasting and rejoicing, a holiday to be celebrated every month and every year. On these days the high priest shall robe himself in the robes of Persia, granted him by my royal personage and by the laws, in honour of the gods and myself and place golden diadems on the statues of my gods, my ancestors and myself.'

King Antiochus Epiphanes I of Commagenes

THE EASTERN region of Turkey is a diverse land which differs profoundly from the rest of the country. The Taurus Mountains in the south and the chain of the Black Sea Mountains in the north encircle the Anatolian Plateau and meet to form a mighty, complex mountain range in the east. Three great axis roads cross the region: the northern highway, which begins in Ankara and reaches the Turco-Iranian frontier via Sivas, Erzincan, Erzurum and Ağrı; the central highway, which extends as far as

114

Lake Van via Kayseri, Malata and Elazığ; and the southern highway, a prolongation of the coastal Mediterranean road, which crosses the High Mesopotamian Plain and follows the borders of Iraq and Syria.

Travellers will be amazed by the variety of the landscape: the red ochre plateau of Erzurum; the forests, waterfalls and green pastures of Kars and Ağrı; the never-melting snow on the Biblical Mount Ağrı; the immense Lake Van with its deep blue waters; the torrid plain of High Mesopotamia; and the fertile valleys of the Dicle and Fırat. Even dwellings and mode of life vary greatly: in the villages of the Kars region are small dwellings built close to the ground; there are lovely terraced houses of the Middle Ages in Mardin; and curious, domed dwellings in Harran.

Life in the region is generally austere, so don't come here if you're expecting sophistication in either the standard of hotel accommodation, or restaurants, because you won't find it. It's wise, also, to choose the time of your visit carefully because, due to altitude and lack of sea influence, the climate of Eastern Turkey is one of extremes: hot, dry summers and harsh winters. Even in summer hot days tend to give way to cold nights. The climate is even more extreme in the north-east, where winters are long and bitter and the summers merely warm. At the other end of the scale, the south-east boasts scorching summers and short, mild winters.

Similarly, historic treasures of the region are full of variety: the astounding sanctuary of Antiochus I, with its colossal statues, at Nemrut Dağı; Byzantine monasteries and churches; mausoleums and caravanserais of the Seljuk period; elegant Ottoman mosques; and hilltop fortresses.

So, for the traveller and lover of adventure this fascinating region of Turkey will have a particularly strong appeal.

Erzincan

Located 730 km. from Ankara, this is the principal town of the province and is situated in a fertile plain. A famous battle where the Seljuks were defeated by the Mongols took place near here in 1248. At Aslantepe, 33 km. away, is an Urartu site where magnificent bronze objects – now exhibited in the Ankara Museum – were discovered.

Erzurum

This is the capital of Eastern Anatolia and is situated on a barren plateau at an altitude of 1,900 m. Of ancient origin, Erzurum became a principal centre during the Byzantine period, when it was called Theodosiopolis, and the walls of its Byzantine fortress are in a well-preserved state. The oldest mosque in the town is the Ulu Cami (Grand Mosque, 1179), which has seven wide parallel naves.

Behind the Medrese is the Hatuniye Türbesi (1255) with a magnificently decorated exterior. The most impressive of the three circular mausoleums is the twelfth-century Emir Sultan Türbesi. A road passing through splendid mountain scenery leads to the new winter sports resort of Inis Boğazi, only 6 km. away from Erzurum.

Kars

This grey and rather forbidding town, famous in Turkish history, stands at the foot of an impressive fortress reconstructed by the Seljuks in the twelfth century. Next to the fortress a tenth-century church now houses a museum. East of Kars is the ancient Silk Road. The impressive walls still encircle ruins of mosques and numerous churches. Kars is the centre of a thriving farming community, noted for its butter and other dairy produce.

Ağrı

Ağrı is dominated on the north-east side by Ağrı Dağı, the eternally snow-capped peak of which is the highest in Turkey. Here Noah's Ark is said to have landed after the Flood.

Doğubayazıt

This small town, pleasantly situated on a spur of Ağrı Dağı, is overlooked by the remains of a Seljuk fortress. Only 6 km. away are the spectacular ruins of the Ishak Paşa Palace and Mosque (seventeenth century), standing amid grandiose scenery of jagged peaks.

Malatya

This is a busy, fairly new town, situated in a fertile plain at the foot of mountains. Adjacent to the town museum is a bazaar where an entire row of shops is devoted to copper objects. From Malatya the two small towns which preceded the foundation of the present-day settlement can be visited.

Elazığ

Another 'new' town, founded in the nineteenth century, it stands on a plain at the foot of a mountain. There are several interesting mosques here, and the mountain is crowned by the fortress of the ancient city of Harput.

Tunceli

The town of Tunceli lies on the Elazığ–Erzurum road surrounded by mountains. The fortress of Pertek, which was constructed in the Middle Ages and is in a well-preserved state, stands 31 km. along the road from Elazığ.

Bingöl

The name of the town means 'a thousand lakes', and though there aren't in fact a thousand, there are indeed many glacier lakes in the surrounding mountains. In the town itself are the remains of a medieval fortress.

Muş

The town was founded in the sixth century and the remains of a citadel and caravanserai can be seen, as well as several mosques.

Bitlis

This lively little town stands in the heart of a green oasis. There is a Byzantine citadel with polygonal towers overlooking the town, and several interesting mosques: the Ulu Cami, built in the twelfth century; the Gökmeydanı Mosque, built by the Seljuks; and the sixteenth-century Şerefiye Mosque.

Eski Ahlat

To the north of Lake Van, the largest lake in Turkey, are the ruins of the ghost-town of Eski Ahlat. In the twelfth century this city was the capital of the Moslem state that ruled the Van basin. Of interest are several mausoleums of the Seljuk period.

Akdamar

On a small island in Lake Van stands the tenth-century
Church of the Holy Cross with its outer walls richly
decorated with reliefs.

Van

The city, an ancient fortified place of Urartu origin, is
situated by the lake of the same name in a verdant oasis at
the foot of a rocky peak crowned by an imposing citadel.
Steps carved in the rock lead to the Urarto fortress, and
half way up, there are inscriptions paying homage to Xerxes. In the old city are numerous mosques and mausoleums of the Seljuk and Ottoman periods, and in the new
city a small but interesting archaeological museum.

Hakkari

The road between Van and Hakkari is passable in
summer, though extremely difficult in winter. In the village of Hoşap, 57 km. from Van, is a beautiful seventeenth-century castle. The small town of Hakkari is
situated at an altitude of 1,700 m., and is dominated by a
mediaeval fortress near to which stands a fine medrese.

Kahraman Maraş

This was once the capital of the Hittite State of Gurgum
(twelfth century BC). Inside the citadel is a small archaeological museum displaying Hittite sculptures. The Ulu
Cami and the Taş Medrese are of the fifteenth century.

Mount Nemrut (Nemrut Dağı)

Mount Nemrut is one of the most impressive sites of Eastern Turkey – not simply because of the grandeur of the mountain itself but because it's here that one finds the gigantic funerary sanctuary erected 2,000 years ago for King Antiochus I of Commagenes. The site is best reached from Adıyaman, where a jeep and driver can be hired for the memorable trip to the summit of the mountain, where the sanctuary is situated at an altitude of 2,150 m.

Antiochus I (62–32 BC) was the most renowned monarch of the land of Commagenes, which encompassed what today is the region of Adıyaman, Maraş and Gaziantep. In 72 BC Commagenes was taken under Roman hegemony, but three years later the Roman commander Lucullus allowed the prince of Commagenes, Mithridates I Kallinikos, to bear the title of king.

The monarchs of Commagenes, like the Persian, Macedonian and many Hellenistic monarchs, were regarded as gods and, indeed, considered themselves as such. They were certainly worshipped as gods. This was why Mithridates I and Antiochus I, son of Laodike, had magnificent tumuli built in their names at the summit of Mount Nemrut. It is also why they had their own statues placed among those of the gods on the sacred court, and why Antioch ordered his people to celebrate his birth with feasts and sacrifices every month and every year. The sacred place, covered with enormous statues, was first discovered by the German Marshall H. von Moltke, and later investigated by experts.

The Commagenes dynasty, claiming common ancestry with the Persians on the one hand and Alexander the Great on the other, came to an end in AD 82 when it was annexed by the Roman emperor Vespasian to the Roman province of Syria.

The king who had his tumulus erected on this sacred terrace also placed an inscription tablet on the southern face of the ancient castle, which stated that the capital of

Commagenes was Arsameia, and after describing the city it details the form of religious ceremonies.

Immediately above the inscription, at a height of 3.43 m., was a relief depicting Mithridates I, the father of Antiochus, and Hercules. This relief was studied by J. S. Young, who came to the conclusion that it dated from the year 50 BC.

Adıyaman itself enjoyed its most brilliant age between the years 69–43 BC, coinciding with King Antiochus' reign.

In the city the remains of a castle built by the Arabs and later restored by the Turks, as well as the fourteenth-century Ulu Cami, may be seen. Many interesting and attractive handicrafts and carpets are on display at Adıyaman Market.

From Nemrut Dağı there is a winding, 85 km. road to Karadut Köyü. After passing Kahta, one should stop at **Eski Kahta** (Old Kahta), 135 km. from Adıyaman. On this road stands the Karakuş (Black Bird) funerary monument erected on behalf of the royal family of Commagenes. On the tumulus is a Roman column surrounded by an eagle. Here, a surviving Roman bridge, the Cendere Köprüsü, crosses the river Kahta.

HOW TO GET TO MOUNT NEMRUT
By air to Diyarbakır and from there by bus to Adıyaman. There are also bus connections from such centres as Istanbul and Ankara.

Gaziantep

This town is quite modern in appearance but is actually of ancient origin. It is the centre of pistachio nut cultivation in Turkey. In the town is a Seljuk fortress and a medrese which now houses an interesting archaeological museum. The artisans of Gaziantep specialize in metalwork.

Urfa

Situated in the great plain of High Mesopotamia, Urfa is one of the most ancient cities in history. In the second century BC it was the capital of a Hurrite State. It is traditionally believed that Abraham stayed here on his way from Ur to the Land of Canaan. Of interest are the remains of a Crusader castle, at the foot of which stands the lovely Halil Rahman Mosque next to a pool of sacred carp. On the other side of the pool is the Ottoman-period Rizvaniye Mosque.

Harran

This village, with its curious domed dwellings, is believed to be the ancient city of Charan mentioned in the Book of Genesis, where Abraham spent several years of his life. There are few remains at Harran: an enclosure, gates, a citadel and the ruins of a very ancient Ommeyyade Mosque.

Diyarbakır

A lively town situated on a plateau close to the banks of the river Tigris. The triple black basalt walls that encircle the old town give it a medieval aspect. These ramparts, which have sixteen keeps and five gates, are among the longest in the world, and are fine examples of the military architecture of the Middle Ages. Also of interest in the town is the Ulu Cami, notable for its original architecture and the number of ancient materials used in the restoration of the building at various times.

Mardin

Whereas Diyarbakır is a city of black appearance due to the basalt used in the old walls, Mardin is a city of white aspect because of its limestone buildings. It stands on a hillslope and overlooks the vast Mesopotamian Plain. Of interest in the city are the ancient citadel and a few beautiful Islamic monuments. Only 7 km. from Mardin, on the road to Akıncı, lies the great Jacobite monastery of **Deyrulzaferan**.

HOW TO GET TO EASTERN TURKEY
By Air   Turkish Airlines operates daily flights to Erzurum from Istanbul, (1 hr. 40 min.), and from Ankara (70 min.) daily except Sundays. The airline also serves Elazığ, Malatya, Diyarbakır and Van from Ankara, plus Van from Diyarbakır.

By Train   The Eastern Express operates daily services between Istanbul–Erzurum–Kars; and Istanbul–Mus–Tatvan and on by ferry to Van. You could also take the Southern Express rail link which leaves Istanbul four times a week for Sivas, Malatya, Maraş or Gaziantep.

By Bus   There are inexpensive daily coach services from both Istanbul and Ankara to all the major towns in the region.

HOTELS AND RESTAURANTS
As mentioned earlier, Eastern Turkey possesses only the most basic hotel accommodation, the majority without modern comforts and facilities. The most acceptable establishments tend to be located in Adıyaman, Doğubayazıt, Erzurum and Van.

USEFUL ADDRESSES

Tourism Bureaux
Erzurum: Cemal Gürsel Cad. Tel. 15 697 -19127
Kars: Ortakapı Mah, Faikbey Cad. İnönü Karakolu Karşısı. Tel. 2724
Malatya: Sivas Cad. No. 5/1. Tel. 17 733
Urfa: Asfaltyol No. 3/D. Tel. 2467
Van: Cumhuriyet Cad. No. 127. Tel. 2018 -3675

Turkish Airlines
Elazığ: Şehit Ilhanlar Cad. 26. Tel. 11 576
Erzurum: Hastaneler Cad. 30 Evler 26/B. Tel. 18 530
Malatya: Dörtyol Halep Cad. 1. Tel. 11 920
Van: Perihanoğlu Iş Merkezi Cumhuriyet Cad. 196. Tel. 1241

Food and Drink

According to many experts on the subject of food, there are only three distinct cuisines in the world: French, Chinese and Turkish, and all the others are derivatives of these. Certainly throughout history the Turkish people have placed great emphasis on the proper preparation of food – and take great delight in creating feasts not only for the palate but also for the eye.

While a visitor to Turkey can enjoy excellent international fare at any good hotel, the most memorable and enjoyable meals are likely to be those taken at the ordinary, everyday restaurants used by Turkish people themselves, offering simple but tasty dishes for moderate prices. At most roadside restaurants you'll find delicious lamb being roasted on revolving spits, salads with tasty dressings and fresh vegetables stuffed with savoury rice. And if you can't understand the names of the dishes – even with the help of this book – you can always go to the kitchen and choose from the pots!

So, what culinary delights are you likely to encounter? Well, a typical meal in a typical restaurant is likely to begin with *meze* or appetizers consisting of white cheese, melon and a mixture of hazel nuts, peanuts and roasted chick peas. The selection might also include *arnavut ciğeri* (small chunks of liver fried and served cold with onions and parsley), *midye dolması* (mussels stuffed with rice, pine nuts and currants), *midye pilakisi* (stewed mussels), pickles and tuna fish. Then there's *sirkeli ceviz sosu* (a mixture of crushed walnuts and vinegar), shrimp cocktail, *cacık* (yoghurt and chopped cucumbers), *pilaki* (a cold dish of stewed white or red beans in olive oil), *dolma* (stuffed vine or cabbage leaves, served cold in olive oil), *beyaz sos* (a mixture of butter, flour, eggs, pepper, lemon juice and coconut), and *zeytinyağlı sarmısak ezmesı* (garlic paste in olive oil).

If you think this is a meal in itself, you're underestimating the appetites of Turkish people, for this is only the beginning. As you clink your glasses of *rakı* – a distillation of grape mash flavoured with aniseed – which is the national drink, popularly known as 'lion's milk', you're likely to be presented with the fish list, offering a tempting selection of such dishes as poached turbot in a rich mayonnaise; baked brill; poached sea bass; swordfish; pike cooked on a skewer; turbot; red mullet; moray eel; anchovies prepared in numerous ways; grilled bluefish; small fried rouget mullets; stuffed mackerel; and those indispensable fruits of the sea, octopus, squid, crab, shrimps, oysters, mussels and lobster.

To accompany any of these dishes you can choose one of the reasonable Turkish red or white wines, good local beer – or, of course, carry on drinking rakı.

Just as the variety of fish dishes is enormous, so too is the choice of meat dishes, especially kebab. Among the types of kebab possessing names of local places, the best known are spicy *Adana* kebab and *Urfa* kebab. Dishes found nationwide include *şiş* kebab, *bahçıvan* kebab (a meat and fresh vegetable stew), *güveç* (mutton or lamb, onions, tomatoes and green peppers), and *talaş* kebab (mutton or lamb, onions and spices) and *döner* kebab.

Other famous accompaniments at your Turkish dinner table might include salads, various soups (*düğün,* yoghurt and *tarhana* to name but three), varieties of *köfte* (ground meat patties too numerous to list), and finally that masterpiece of pastry art the *börek,* made from thin slices of filo pastry filled variously with cheese, spinach, chicken, ground meat and vegetables and cooked in every conceivable shape and form. You may also find *çerkez tavuğu,* or Circassian chicken, which is chicken served in a thick sauce made from walnuts.

Turkish desserts are certainly not designed for weight-watchers but are truly delicious. Along with fresh fruit – among the freshest you're ever likely to taste – there's often a choice of such specialities as yoghurt cakes, *helva*, various puddings such as *revani* or *güllaç*, or sweet pastries such as *kadayıf, bülbül yuvası, hanım göbeği* or *dilber dudağı.*

To drink, there's mineral water in capped bottles (*maden suyu*), beer (*bira*), Turkish wines, red (*kirmizi şarap*), or white (*beyaz şarap*) and soft drinks such as *Fruko*, which is bitter lemon. Fruit juices of all kinds are also generally available. And if you're ordering Turkish coffee to round off your meal, remember the degrees of sweetness: *şekerli*, very sweet; *orta şekerli*, medium; *az şekerli*, a little sugar. If you don't want sugar, ask for *sade kahve*.

So, *Afiyet olsun* – Bon appetit!

Useful Words and Phrases

The Turkish alphabet is very similar to the Latin alphabet except for a few letters which have special pronunciation:

c = j as in *Cami* (mosque) pronounced Jami
ç = ch as in Foça pronounced Focha
ğ unpronounced but serves to extend the preceding vowel so that Dağ (mountain) is pronounced Daa
ö = oe as in Göreme pronounced Goereme
ş = sh as in Kuşadası pronounced Kushadası
ü = like the French 'tu' as in Ürgüp
ı = pronounced like the 'a' in the English word *'serial'*

EVERYDAY PHRASES

To the words *'hoş geldiniz'* (welcome), you reply *'hoş bulduk'*.

hello   *merhaba*
good-bye   *allahaısmarladık* (said by the person leaving)
            güle güle (said by the person seeing his or her friends off)
good-morning   *günaydın*
good-evening   *iyi akşamlar*
good-night   *iyi geceler*
please   *lütfen*
thank you   *teşekkür ederim* or *mersi*
yes   *evet*
no   *hayır*
there is   *var*
there is not   *yok* (used to express the availability or unavailability of something)
how are you?   *nasılsınız*
I am well, thank you   *iyiyim, teşekkür ederim*

128

NUMBERS

1	*bir*	6	*altı*	11	*on bir*	60	*altmış*	101 *yüz bir*
2	*iki*	7	*yedi*	20	*yirmi*	70	*yetmiş*	200 *iki yüz*
3	*üç*	8	*sekiz*	30	*otuz*	80	*seksen*	300 *üç yüz*
4	*dört*	9	*dokuz*	40	*kırk*	90	*doksan*	1000 *bin*
5	*beş*	10	*on*	50	*elli*	100	*yüz*	2000 *iki bin*

THE TIME AND THE DAYS
when? *ne zaman?*
yesterday *dün*
today *bugün*
tomorrow *yarın*
morning *sabah*
afternoon *öğleden sonra*
evening *akşam*
night *gece*
one hour *bir saat*
what is the time? *saat kaç?*
at what time? *saat kaçta?*
Sunday *Pazar*
Monday *Pazartesi*
Tuesday *Salı*
Wednesday *Çarşamba*
Thursday *Perşembe*
Friday *Cuma*
Saturday *Cumartesi*

WHILE TRAVELLING
airport *hava alanı*
port *liman*
town centre *şehir merkezi*
where is it? *nerede?*
is it far? *uzak mı?*
tourism bureau *turizm bürosu*
repair garage *bir tamirci*
a good hotel *iyi bir otel*
a restaurant *bir lokanta*
attention! *dikkat!*

129

IN THE HOTEL
a room   *bir oda*
two people   *iki kişi*
a room with a bathroom   *banyolu bir oda*
what is the price?   *fiyati nedir?*
hot water   *sıcak su*
a supplementary bed   *ilave bir yatak*
breakfast   *kahvaltı*
butter   *tereyağ*
coffee   *kahve*
tea   *çay*
milk   *süt*
sugar   *şeker*
the bill   *hesap*

AT THE GARAGE
petrol   *benzin*
petrol station   *benzin istasyonu*
oil   *motor yağı*
change of oil   *yağlama*
tyre   *lastik*
brakes   *frenler*
sparking plugs   *bujiler*
it does not work   *çalışmıyor*

SHOPPING
how much is it?   *bu ne kadar?*
it is very expensive   *çok pahalı*
I do not like it   *beğenmedim*
is it old?   *eski mi?*
gold   *altın*
silver   *gümüş*
leather   *deri*
copper   *bakır*

130

IN THE RESTAURANT
bread   *ekmek*
water   *su*
mineral water   *maden suyu*
fruit juice   *meyva suyu*
wine   *şarap*
beer   *bira*
ice   *buz*
meat   *et*
mutton   *koyun eti*
lamb   *kuzu eti*
beef   *sığır eti*
veal   *dana eti*
chicken   *piliç*
fish   *balık*

Hors d'oeuvre *mezeler*
arnavut ciğeri   spicy fried liver with onions
çerkez tavuğu   cold chicken in walnut purée with garlic
çiğ köfte   spicy raw meatballs
tarama   fish-roe salad
yaprak dolması   stuffed vine leaves

Soups *çorbalar*
yoğurt çorbası   yoghurt soup
düğün çorbası   meat soup with egg yolks
işkembe çorbası   tripe soup

Grills *ızgaralar*
bonfile   fillet steak
döner kebap   lamb grilled on a revolving spit
pirzola   lamb chops
şiş kebap   grilled lamb on skewers
şiş köfte   grilled meatballs

Pilafs *pilavlar*
sade pilav   plain rice pilaf
iç pilav   rice with pine nuts, currants and onions
bulgur pilavı   cracked wheat pilaf

Cold vegetables in olive oil *zeytinyağlılar*
imam bayıldı   split aubergine with tomatoes and onions
kabak kızartması   fried baby marrow slices served with
                yoghurt
patlıcan kızartması   fried aubergine slices served with
                yoghurt
zeytinyağlı fasulye   green beans in tomato sauce

Savoury pastries *börekler*
sigara böreği   fried filo pastry filled with cheese
su böreği   layers of filo pastry baked with cheese or meat
          fillings
talaş böreği   puff pastry filled with meat

Salads *salatalar*
cacık   chopped cucumbers in garlic-flavoured yoghurt
çoban salatası   mixed tomato, pepper, cucumber and
                onion salad
patlıcan salatası   puréed aubergine salad
piyaz   haricot bean and onion salad

Desserts *tatlılar*
baklava   flaky pastry stuffed with nuts in syrup
tel kadayıf   shredded wheat stuffed with nuts in syrup
sütlaç   creamy cold rice pudding
komposto   cold stewed fruit
dondurma   ice cream

Fruits *meyvalar*
grapes   *üzüm*
peaches   *şeftali*
plums   *erik*
apricots   *kayısı*
cherries   *kiraz*
figs   *incir*
yellow melon   *kavun*
water melon   *karpuz*

Useful Information

When to go to Turkey

The Marmara, Aegean and Mediterranean coastal regions of Turkey enjoy a typical Mediterranean climate, with hot summers and mild winters. The Black Sea coastal region, too, enjoys warm summers and mild winters, but with relatively high rainfall; while in central and eastern Anatolia, hot dry summers give way to very cold winters. And even in summer the nights are cool, so if you're visiting this part of Turkey, take warm jumpers and cardigans with you.

AVERAGE LAND TEMPERATURES (CENTIGRADE)

	Jan	Apr	Jul	Oct
Marmara region (Istanbul)	5	12	23	16
Aegean region (Izmir)	9	16	28	18
Mediterranean region (Antalya)	11	16	28	20
Black Sea region (Trabzon)	7	12	23	16
Central Anatolia (Ankara)	0	11	23	13
Eastern Anatolia (Erzurum)	−9	5	19	9

AVERAGE SEA TEMPERATURES (CENTIGRADE)

	Jan	Apr	Jul	Oct
Marmara region (Istanbul)	8	11	23	17
Aegean region (Izmir)	11	15	26	21
Mediterranean region (Antalya)	18	18	26	24
Black Sea region (Trabzon)	10	10	24	20

How to Go

BY AIR

Turkish Airlines (THY) operates regular flights to Ankara, Istanbul, Izmir, Antalya and Dalaman airports from the principal capitals and important cities of the world. Most international airlines have daily flights from European capitals to Istanbul's international airport. Services to Ankara's airport are slightly less frequent, but there are THY connecting flights. In addition, a growing number of charter airlines are operating flights to Turkey's Mediterranean and Aegean regions, especially Dalaman Airport in the south, which serves many of the increasingly popular south-coast resorts.

BY SEA

Turkish Maritime Lines has regular passenger ferry services to Turkish ports from Ancona and Magosa. Apart from the numerous cruises in the Mediterranean, several foreign shipping companies have regular services to the ports of Istanbul, Izmir and Kuşadası.

BY RAIL

From Venice   Daily departures for Istanbul by the 'Istanbul Express' via Trieste, Belgrade and Sofia, arriving Istanbul on the morning of the third day. Wagon-lits services available twice weekly.

From Munich   Two daily services for Istanbul by the 'Istanbul Express' and the 'Tauern–Orient Express' via Salzburg, Zagreb, Belgrade, Sofia.

From Vienna   Daily services for Istanbul by the 'Istanbul Express' and the Balkan Express via Graz, Zagreb, Belgrade, Sofia. A Bulgarian transit visa is necessary.

BY ROAD

By Coach   There are regular coach services between Turkey and Austria, France, Germany and Switzerland, also Iraq, Jordan, Saudi Arabia and Syria.

By Private Car The London–Istanbul journey is approximately 3,000 km. Route: Calais or Ostend to Brussels, Cologne and Frankfurt; from Frankfurt there are two alternative routes. (1) Nuremberg, Linz, Vienna, Budapest, Zagreb, Belgrade. (2) Stuttgart, Munich, Salzburg, Ljubljana, Zagreb, Belgrade and from Belgrade to Nis, Sofia, Edirne and Istanbul. One can also use the car ferry from Venice or Ancona by driving south from Munich to Italy.

MARITIME LINES BETWEEN TURKEY AND GREECE

Çeşme–Chios (ferry boats) Three services a week from the beginning of June to mid-July; one service daily from the middle of July to 1 September. Crossing time: 1 hr.

Kuşadası–Samos (boats and speedboards) Several daily services starting 1 May. Crossing by boat takes about two hours. Most of the boats can take only a couple of cars.

Bodrum–Cos (boat) Everyday except Sundays. Crossing time: 1 hr. 30 min.

Marmaris–Rhodes (boats and ferry boats) Services every day in both directions except Sundays. Crossing time: 3 hr. 30 min.

Reductions There are reductions for return tickets and also for students, teachers, journalists, families and groups.

PASSPORTS AND VISAS

Nationals of the following countries require a valid passport only (without visa) for stays of up to three months: Australia, Austria, Bahamas, Bahrain, Barbados, Belgium, Canada, Denmark, Fiji Isles, Finland,

France, Gambia, Federal Republic of Germany, Gibraltar, Greece, Grenada, Hong Kong, Iran, Iceland, Ireland, Italy, Jamaica, Japan, Kenya, Kuwait, Liechtenstein, Luxemburg, Mauritius, Malta, Monaco, Morocco, Seychelles, Spain, Switzerland, Trinidad and Tobago, Tunisia, Turkish Republic of Northern Cyprus, Uganda, United Arab Emirates, United Kingdom, USA, Vatican.

Nationals of the following countries require a valid passport only (without visa) for stays of up to two months: Portugal, Romania, Yugoslavia, South Korea.

Nationals of Malaysia may stay for up to 15 days without a visa upon production of a valid passport.

Nationals of all other countries require visas, which can be obtained from the nearest Turkish Embassy or Consulate.

Currency Regulations

Limits   There is no limit on the amount of foreign currency that may be brought into Turkey, but not more than US $1,000 worth of Turkish currency may be brought into or taken out of the country.

Exchange Slips   The exchange slips for the conversion of foreign currency into Turkish lira should be kept, since you will be required to show these when reconverting your Turkish lira back into foreign currency and when taking foreign currency out of the country (to prove it has been purchased with legally exchanged foreign currency). You can change money at banks and authorized hotels at the official rate of exchange.

Where to Stay

HOTEL ACCOMMODATION

In recent years – especially since the early 1960s when a national plan was devised and carried out by the Ministry of Culture and Tourism – Turkey has made considerable strides forward in the field of hotel development. It should be noted, however, that hotel establishments are unequally distributed throughout the country, that there are few international-standard luxury hotels considering its size, and that at the typical hotel which the visitor will encounter, the facilities and amenities are likely to fall considerably short of many other popular holiday destinations.

The best hotels are to be found, not surprisingly, in Turkey's three major cities, Istanbul, Ankara and Izmir. Excellent establishments are also located in the environs of Istanbul, such as the coastal regions of the Sea of Marmara; the Mediterranean coast – Antalya, Side, Alanya, Mersin and Adana; and certain other tourist regions such as Cappadocia, Konya and Pamukkale.

In all other regions the number of hotels corresponding to Western standards is disappointingly small, although considerable development of stylish and well-equipped hotels and holiday villages is well under way in the fast-developing holiday resorts of the Mediterranean and Aegean coasts.

A certain number of hotels throughout Turkey are registered with the Ministry of Culture and Tourism, and figure in most of the literature and guides produced by the Ministry. They are selected on the basis of certain standards of facilities, and generally offer a reasonable degree of comfort and cleanliness. However, just because an establishment is not listed by the Ministry does not mean it isn't worth considering, since certain criteria are somewhat arbitrary.

Apart from Cappadocia, Konya and Pamukkale, don't expect to find sophisticated hotels in Turkey's interior because, as yet, they exist in only very small numbers;

the majority are, at best, modest – and, at worst, basic.

There are still very few guest houses in Turkey, and private lodging with families is little done – or, at any rate, seldom organized. However, it would be difficult to find a Turk who could be accused of being inhospitable, and if the opportunity arises Turkish people often extend their hospitality to travellers in search of a place to stay the night.

CAMPING

The camping grounds registered with the Ministry of Culture and Tourism are still few in number, but they are all situated on the principal routes, near towns and tourist centres. The camping sites of the Mocamp Kervansaray chain, modern-day equivalents of the old caravanserais, are very comfortable and often have restaurants and occasionally chalets with rooms – and some have private beaches. The grounds managed by this company guarantee a good reception for caravaners and campers. The camping sites are generally open from April or May until October, and though camping on other than official sites is possible, it is not really advisable.

How to Travel in Turkey

BY AIR

Turkish Airlines provides an important network of domestic Turkish flights from the airports of Istanbul, Ankara and Izmir to all the major Turkish cities. However, the airline does not enjoy the best of reputations for sticking closely to published timetables, so check in advance with a travel agent or a THY office whenever possible. It's also advisable to check in early, as flights are often fully booked.

Transfers   There are regular coach transfers to and from airports and city centres in Istanbul, Ankara and Izmir.

BY SEA

Turkish Maritime Lines operates several coastal services which provide excellent sightseeing possibilities. All the services depart from the Eminönü or Karaköy sides of Istanbul's Galata Bridge, and early bookings for the touristic cruises is advised because they are in heavy demand.

Istanbul Services

Boğaziçi (Bosphorus) car ferry: Kabataş (European side) – Üşküdar (Asian side), departing from both sides every 15 min., the crossing taking 15 min.
Boğaziçi tour: departing from Eminönü and zigzagging up the Bosphorus to Anadolu Kavağı.
Princes' Islands service: Eminönü–Büyükada (largest of the islands), crossing in 1½ hr.

Marmara car ferries

Kartal (20 km. outside Istanbul on the Asian side)–Yalova (south coast of Marmara), crossings from both sides frequently in 1 hr. 40 min.
Istanbul–Mudanya–Gemlik and Istanbul–Bandırma: one service per week.
Çanakkale Boğazı (Dardanelles) ferries: Gelibolu (European side)–Lapseki (Asian side): crossing once every two hours from each side: and Eceabat (European side)–Çanakkale (Asian side), crossing once every two hours from each side in 30 min.

Marmara sea services

Istanbul–Mudanya: all year, Fridays, departing Istanbul 09.00 hrs. In summer season Sundays also, departing 09.00 hrs.
Istanbul–Avşa: every day in July and August, departing Istanbul 08.30 hrs. Extra service Fridays, departing Istanbul 17.30 hrs.
Istanbul–Bandırma: all year, every day, departing Istanbul 08.30 hrs.
Istanbul–Karabiga: (via Saraylar Köyü, Marmara, Avşa),

every Wednesday, with Saturday service in summer, departing 09.30 hrs.

Istanbul–Gemlik: all year, Fridays, with Sunday services in the summer. Departs Istanbul 09.00 hrs.

Mediterranean cruise
Istanbul–Alanya–Istanbul line: a ten-day cruise with stops in Izmir, Kuşadası, Gülük, Bodrum, Datça, Marmaris, Fethiye, Antalya and Alanya. One service a week in summer. Departs from Istanbul each Wednesday at 14.00 hrs.

Black Sea cruise
Istanbul–Trabzon–Istanbul line: a six-day cruise operating weekly and stopping in Sinop, Samsun, Giresun and Trabzon.

Reductions 10 per cent on return tickets. No charge for children up to the age of four, and 50 per cent reductions for children from 4 to 12, students and journalists. (There are no reductions no meal prices.)

Formalities for Motorists

Cars, minibuses, caravans, towed sea-craft, motorcycles and bicycles can be brought into Turkey for up to three months without a *'Carnet de Passage'* or *'triptique'*. The vehicle is simply registered in the owner's passport and this registration is cancelled when the owner leaves the country. For stays longer than three months it is necessary to apply to the Turkish Touring and Automobile Club for a *'triptique'*. If a tourist wishes to visit another country from Turkey without his car he should take the vehicle to the nearest Customs Authority (*Gümrük Müdürlüğü*) so that the registration of the car in his passport may be cancelled. Drivers need a three-sectioned driving licence or an international driving licence.

INSURANCE

A motorist should have either:

(a) Green Card international insurance, endorsed for Turkish territory both in Europe and Asia; or

(b) Turkish third-party insurance, which can be taken out from any of the insurance agencies at the frontier posts.

IN CASE OF AN ACCIDENT

Whether or not anyone is injured, the police should be notified as a report is essential.

If you hold a credit cheque from your own automobile association, the Turkish Touring and Automobile Association (*Türkiye Turing ve Otomobil Kurumu*) will carry out necessary repairs and forward the bill to your own country.

If you own an A.I.T. or an F.I.A. assistance booklet, the Turkish Touring and Automobile Association will bear the cost of transporting your damaged vehicle from the scene of the accident to the Customs, and thence to your home.

If it is necessary to leave a vehicle in Turkey after an accident for eventual collection, the vehicle must be delivered to a Customs Office so that the vehicle's endorsement on your passport may be deleted. Without this deletion it is not possible to leave the country! When leaving a vehicle at the Customs it should be made clear that this is a temporary measure. It should be noted that any vehicle not claimed within three months is considered to have been abandoned.

If your vehicle is totally wrecked and you wish to abandon it in Turkey, it should be taken to the nearest Customs Office. If there isn't one nearby, then you should contact the local administrative authority (*Mülki Amirlik*) to arrange for the vehicle to be sent to a Customs Office. The latter will then cancel the endorsement of your vehicle in your passport and you will be free to leave the country.

If your vehicle is stolen it is necessary to obtain a certificate from the governor of the province (*Vali*) so that the vehicle's endorsement on your passport can be cancelled before leaving the country.

The Road Network

The 26,000 km. of asphalt highways are reasonably well maintained and quite easy to drive on. The roads denoted as 'stabilized' are of gravel chippings laid ready for asphalt. Coming from Europe, the crossing of the Bosphorus to Asia has been greatly speeded up by the completion of the Istanbul bypass and the Boğaziçi Bridge, leading to the Istanbul–Izmit express road (now completed up to Gebze). The three great axis roads traversing Turkey are those to Syria and the Lebanon (E 5), Iraq (E 24) and Iran (E 23). In winter certain passes such as the Tahir Pass (2,475 m.) between Erzurum and Ağrı, and the Kopdağı Pass (2,390 m.) between Trabzon and Aşkale are sometimes closed due to heavy snowfall. Another main pass is the Zigana Pass at 2,025 m. on the Trabzon–Gümüşhane road.

ROAD SIGNS
Turkish road signs conform to the International Protocol on Road Signs. Archaeological and historic sites are indicated by yellow signposts.

Car Repairs

There are numerous repair garages in towns (usually grouped together along certain streets) and along main roads. While there are official agents in Ankara, Izmir and, of course, Istanbul that deal in spare parts for foreign makes of cars, it is advisable to make sure your car has been thoroughly overhauled and serviced before taking it to Turkey, since spare parts are often unavailable.

Road Rescue Services
(located on the E5 Edirne–Ankara road)

Edirne   Tel. 1170
Babaeski = 57 km. from Edirne
Çorlu = 75 km. from Babaeski
Silivri = 42 km. from Çorlu
Küçükçekmece = 40 km. from Silivri
Istanbul   Tel. 353 35 11
Izmit. Tel. 2330 = 66 km. from Istanbul
Sakarya. Tel. 135 94 = 46 km. from Izmit
Boludağ. Tel. 3723 = 92 km. from Sakarya
Esentepe = 70 km. from Boludağ
Çamlıdere = 28 km. from Esentepe
Pınar = 41 km. from Çamlıdere
Ankara   Tel. 15 83 38

In addition, assistance can be called for from the Touring and Automobile Club: Istanbul head office. Tel. 146 70 90; Ankara office, Tel. 18 65 78

ROAD MAPS
The General Directorate of Highways and the Ministry of Culture and Tourism annually publish free road maps (1/1,850,000) on which historic sites and other points of interest are indicated.

TRAFFIC CIRCULATION
Traffic circulates on the right, and the Turkish Highway Code is similar to those of West European countries. Outside the major cities traffic moves quite freely, the Istanbul–Ankara highway being the only one on which traffic is particularly heavy. There is a 50 kph speed limit in urban centres and a 90 kph limit out of town.

PETROL
Petrol prices are generally below those of many European countries, though there are slight variations depending on the nearness of a filling station to a refi-

nery. And certainly outside the major cities and towns, petrol stations can be few and far between, so it's best to fill up when you can. The brands of petrol available are: Petrol Ofisi, Türk Petrol, BP, Mobil and Shell. 'Super' grades of petrol can be found all over the country except in the most isolated parts.

Formalities for Private Yacht Owners

Yachts require a Transit Log, and may remain in Turkish waters for up to two years for maintenance or for wintering. There are certain ports licensed by the Ministry of Culture and Tourism for the storage of yachts for a period of two years. Upon arriving in Turkish waters, yachts should immediately go for control of the ship's log to the nearest port of entry, which are as follows: Çanakkale, Bandırma, Istanbul, Akçay, Ayvalık, Dikili, Izmir, Çeşme, Kuşadası, Güllük, Bodrum, Datça, Marmaris, Fethiye, Kaş, Antalya, Alanya, Anamur, Taşucu (Silifke), Mersin and Iskenderun.

Formalities on Reaching Port   All the required information concerning the yacht, yachtsmen, crew members, intended route, passports, customs declarations, health clearance and any other obligatory matters must be entered in the Transit Log. The latter is to be completed by the captain of a yacht under a foreign flag, or by an amateur sailor acting as captain of the vessel. The Transit Log must be completed upon first entering a Turkish port, and generally no further formalities are required until departure. Before leaving, Section V is to be completed for the Customs Authorities.

Formalities for Private Aircraft Owners

When coming to Turkey, international air lanes should be followed. Private aircraft may stay for up to three months in Turkey with tourist status; for longer periods permission should be obtained from the Ministry of Customs and Monopolies (*Gümrük ve Tekel Bakanlığı, Ankara*). For further information apply to the Civil Aviation Department of the Ministry of Transport (*Ulaştırma Bakanlığı, Sivil Havacılık Dairesi, Ankara*).

Customs Regulations

ON ENTRY
The following items may be brought into the country duty free:
—personal effects of the tourists
—clothing and personal decorative items (but not furs)
—books, magazines and one portable typewriter
—personal sporting equipment
—one musical instrument
—one camera and up to ten rolls of film
—one transistor radio and amateur compass
—necessary medical items
—400 cigarettes, 50 cigars, 200 g. tobacco, 1 kg. coffee, 500 g. instant coffee, 1 kg. tea and five bottles of spirits of which no more than three shall be of the same brand.
Valuable items must be registered in the owner's passport for control upon exit.
Sharp instruments (including camping knives) and weapons may not be brought into the country without special permission.
Taking into the country marijuana and all other narcotics is strictly forbidden and subject to heavy punishment.
Antiques brought into the country must be registered in the owner's passport to avoid difficulties on exit.

ON EXIT
Gifts and souvenirs up to the value of 15,000 TL may be taken out of Turkey. However, for a new carpet a proof of purchase is necessary, and for old items a certificate from a director of a museum is essential.

145

Antiques cannot be exported from Turkey.
Valuable personal items can be taken out of the country only if they have been registered in the owner's passport, or providing the owner can show they have been purchased with legally exchanged currency.
Minerals may be exported only with a special document obtained from the General Directorate of Mining Exploration and Research.

Health Regulations for Animals

Domestic animals and hunting dogs must have a rabies vaccination certificate issued 48 hrs. before departure, and this should have been translated into Turkish by a Turkish Embassy or Consulate.

Geography

Throughout history Turkey's geographical position has had a profound influence on world events. Situated mainly in Asia Minor, with a foothold in the Balkans, Turkey lies neither completely in Asia nor Europe, yet has been both a link and a frontier zone between the two continents. In this situation it has influenced and been influenced by events in both Europe and the Middle East.

Turkey lies in the North Hemisphere near the centre of the 'Old World' continents i.e. Asia, Africa, and Europe. More specifically, it lies near the Western and Central part of the European and North African countries. Turkey also occupies a middle position between the North Pole and Equator.

Turkey's territory is roughly in the shape of a rectangle measuring 550 km. from north to south and 1,565 km. from east to west at its widest points. The country is situated in an area of 779,452 sq. km. of which 755,688 sq. km. lie in that part of Asia known as Asia Minor or *Anadolu* (Anatolia), and 23,764 in that part of Europe known as *Trakya* (Eastern Thrace). The two islands of *Imroz* (Imbros) and *Bozcaada* (Tenedos), lying in the Aegean Sea on either side of the mouth of the *Çanakkale Boğazı* (Dardanelles), also belong to Turkey.

The two continents, Europe and Asia, are separated by the Straits, consisting, from south-west to north-east, of the *Çanakkale Boğazı* (the Dardanelles), *Marmara Denizi* (the Sea of Marmara) and *Boğaziçi* (Bosphorus). With its geographically important position, its vast land mass, and its constantly increasing population, Turkey is a powerful entity and a valuable element of balance in this part of the world.

TOPOGRAPHY

The geological evolution of Turkey, which is on the Alpine–Himalayan mountain range, started towards the end of the 'First Era' and ended in the 'Fourth Era'. It is a country of high elevation, with an average altitude of 1,130 m. Mountain ranges extend from the west to the east along the northern and southern coasts of the country, and there are also many plains, plateaux, highlands and basins.

Topographically, Turkey is divided into five regions, Northern, Southern, Eastern, Western and Central Anatolia – each of which displays different characteristics.

Northern Anatolia   Folding mountains of various altitudes which may be considered as lying in successive ranges all along the northern coast roughly enframe Northern Anatolia along the Black Sea coast. Their appearance is deformed in the west, beginning in the lower section of the Sakarya River. Further west there are the medium-high Yıldız Mountains (Istranca). The eastern sections of the Northern Anatolian mountains are steep, with altitudes ranging from 3,000 to 4,000 m. The highest of these are the Eastern Black Sea mountains and the Giresun mountains, covering the area between the Çoruh River and the Melet Valley. Kaçkar Peak is the highest point at 3,937 m. In this region, the Zigana Pass (2,025 m.), between Trabzon and Gümüşhane, and the Mount Kop Pass (2,309 m.) between Bayburt and Aşkale, are the main routes between the coast and Central Anatolia.

Southern Anatolia   *Toros Dağları,* the Taurus Mountains in Southern Anatolia longitudinally cover the entire southern part of the country, and resemble the Southern Alpine system; however, the folded Taurus Mountains appear in more than one range. These lengthy ranges have internal and external arches, the external arch being in the Hakkari mountains in south-eastern Turkey, extending towards Siirt, Ergani and north of Kahramanmaraş. Turkey's highest mountains rise in the Hakkari region. Beginning from the east there are Sat Mountain, Cilo Mountain and Karadağ Mountain, all of which have a varying elevation of 3,000 to 4,000 m.

The interior arches of the Taurus Mountains are located mainly north of Çukurova. They extend in ranges between Taşeli and the Uzunyayla highlands, and reach an altitude of more than 3,000 m. The western section of the Taurus arches appears as ranges lying on both sides of the Gulf of Antalya and meeting at the 'Lake District'.

Eastern Anatolia   Surrounded by the Northern Anatolian mountain ranges and the Southern Taurus arches, Eastern Anatolia is Turkey's highest region. The Munzur Mountains, which form the Karasu–Aras arch, reach an altitude of 3,500 m., starting from the south of Erzincan, and extend to Erzurum's Palandöken Mountains and Aras plain, with their highest peaks at Mount Ağrı (5,165 m.) and Küçük Ağrı (3,925 m.).

Central Anatolia   This region is less mountainous compared with the others, the average altitude being between 1,000 and 2,000 m.

Western Anatolia   The Mountains here extend towards

the Aegean Sea. The highest peaks include Emirdağı
(2,214 m.), Türkmen Mountain, Mount Domaniç, Mount
Uludağ (the ancient Olympus – 2,543 m.), Sandıklı
Mountains and Mount Murat (2,312 m.). In the north, the
Kocaeli and Çatalca peninsulas are mountainous. On the
European side of Turkey is the Yıldız mountain range,
which forms the start of the Northern mountain range.

Seas and Coasts

Turkey is surrounded by the sea on three sides, with
more than 8,000 km. of coastline. The Anatolian coast
along the Black Sea is of high elevation in most areas,
with mountain ranges lying directly parallel to the coast.
The main inlets are: Sinop, Samsun, Amasra and the Ereğli between Ordu, Ünye, Trabzon and Vakfıkebir.
Situated between the Black, Aegean and Mediterranean
seas are Boğaziçi (Bosphorus Strait), the Sea of Marmara
and Çanakkale (Dardanelles Strait). The Sea of Marmara
is a small, internal sea between two straits, the Bosphorus and the Dardanelles. Its islands are located in the
shallow parts, the largest being the Marmara Islands.
The Dardanelles Strait extends between Gelibolu (the
ancient Gallipoli) and the Biga Peninsulas. On Turkey's
Aegean coast there are numerous peninsulas, capes,
gulfs, inlets and bays of various sizes, while several
rivers empty into the sea on this coast, forming deltas.
The continental shelf of the Mediterranean coast of Turkey is narrow, and is formed by steep cliffs along its full
length. The Taurus range lies paralled to the sea, and the
two main inlets are the Gulfs of Antalya and Iskenderun.

Population

Turkey has 46 million inhabitants, 57 per cent of whom
live in the countryside. The population density is
greatest in the western coastal regions. The major cities

are Istanbul (4,000,000), Ankara, the capital, (3,000,000), Izmir (2,000,000), Adana (1,500,000) and Konya (1,500,000).

Language

The Turkish language is neither Indo-European nor Semitic, but a language on its own. In Turkey the language is written with Latin characters, but Turkish is in fact spoken by a total of some 85 million people and other scripts are used outside Turkey.

Economy

Agriculture   This plays a very important role in the Turkish economy. The main crops are wheat, cotton, tobacco and fruit. Sheep are Turkey's most important livestock, and Turkey is the major European wool producer.

Natural Resources   The principal minerals extracted are coal, chrome (an important export), iron, copper, bauxite, sulphur and oil.

Industry   Industry is developing rapidly and is directed mainly towards the processing of agricultural products, metallurgy, textiles and the manufacture of automobiles and agricultural machinery.

Where to Obtain Information

For all information concerning a trip to Turkey contact your nearest Turkish Tourism and Information Bureau abroad and you will be provided with brochures, road maps and hotel guides, etc. In Turkey there are information bureaux in all the principal cities and tourist centres.

Postal System and Phone Calls

Turkish post offices are easily recognizable by their yellow 'PTT' signs. Major post offices are open 08.00 to 24.00 hrs. Monday–Saturday and 09.00 to 19.00 hrs. on Sunday. Small post offices have the same opening hours as government offices (see below).

POST RESTANTE
Post restante letters should be addressed *'posterestant'* to the central post office, *Merkez Postanesı*, in the town of your choice. It is necessary to produce an identification card when collecting your letter.

PHONE CALLS
Within a City   You buy a token at a post office to slot into the machine as soon as the dialled number answers.

Inter-City   Direct dialling is becoming a little more commonplace in Turkey these days, especially in the major cities and tourist centres. Elsewhere, it is necessary to request the call at a post office. Officially, calls can be *normal, acele* (urgent) or *yıldırım* (very urgent), but you can still be kept waiting even with the latter!

Opening Times

Government Offices   08.30–12.30, 13.30–17.30, closed Saturdays and Sundays.

Banks   09.00–13.00, 14.00–19.00, closed Saturdays and Sundays.

Shops   09.00–13.00, 14.00–19.00, closed Sundays. Many smaller shops, however, keep longer hours and do not close for lunch.

Summer Hours   In the Aegean and Mediterranean

regions government offices and many other establishments are closed during the afternoons in the summer months. These summer hours are fixed each year by the relevant provincial governors.

Official Holidays

January 1   New Year's Day
April 23   National Independence Children's Day
May 19   Atatürk's Commemoration and Youth and
  Sports Day
August 30   Victory Day
October 29   Republic Day (anniversary of the declaration of the Turkish Republic)

National Parks

Uludağ (Mount Olympus of Mysia)   Located near Bursa at a height of 2,554 m., the region contains impressive forests and lakes, and is ideal for summer picnics and walks. Winter sports are available from December to April, and there's hotel accommodation for visitors, as well as camping sites.

Kuşcenneti (Bird Paradise)   An ornithological reserve containing more than two hundred species of birds, it is located in the province of Balıkesir, on Highway 15. The most interesting seasons to visit the reserve are March to July and September to October.

Sipil Dağı   Situated in Manisa Province, on the E23, it's an area rich in interesting flora, fauna and thermal springs. The best season for a visit is from April to November, when camping and picnicking are possible.

Dilek Yarımadası (Peninsula)   In the province of Aydın, on the E24, 30, where Mount Samandağı plunges to the sea, is an area of river valleys, beaches, bays and cliffs, noted for its interesting flora and fauna.

Kovada   An excellent region for water sports, fishing and picnics, Kovada is situated in Isparta Province, on the E24.

Düzler Çamı   Wild scenery, flora and fauna greet the visitor to this region of Antalya, on the E24. In the same direction is the Olympus–Beydağları, forested mountains where the ancient sites of Phaselis and Olympus are located.

Karatepe–Aslantaş   Situated in the river Ceyhan Valley, Adana Province, on the E5, 47, the region is noted for its hills, valleys and flora, as well as Hittite and Roman remains.

Munzur Vadisi (Valley)   There are streams full of trout, natural springs, and rich flora and fauna in this valley located in the province of Tunceli, on the E391.

Yozgat Çamlığı   Forests, green hills and valleys, flora and fauna are the attractions of this region of Yozgat province, on Highway E23.

Soğuksu   Situated in Ankara province in the E5, near Kızılcahamam, with its thermal springs and forested plateau cut by small valleys, Soğuksu has an hotel and restaurant, camping and picnic spots.

Ilgaz Dağı   A beautiful landscape in the province of Kastamonu, on Highway 39.

Yedigöller ('Seven Lakes')   This region of Zonguldak province on the E5, 35, boasts beautiful forests and fish-filled lakes.

Religious Holidays

There are two main religious holidays in Islam. Firstly, the three-day *Şeker Bayramı* (Sugar Festival) when sweets are eaten to celebrate the end of the fast of Ramadan; secondly, the four-day *Kurban Bayramı* (Festival of Sacrifices), when sacrificial sheep are killed and their meat distributed to the poor. The dates of these festivals change according to the Moslem calendar, and during the festivals shops and government offices are closed.

Folk Traditions

FOLK MUSIC

The lively Turkish folk music, which originated on the steppes of Asia, is in complete contrast to the refined Turkish classical music of the Ottoman court.

Until recently folk music was not written down, and the traditions have been kept alive by the *aşıklar* (troubadours). Distinct from the folk music is the Ottoman military music and the religious music of the Whirling Dervishes. The solemn military music, now performed by the *mehter takımı* (Janissary Band) in Istanbul, originated in Central Asia and is played with kettle drums, clarinets, cymbals and bells. The mystical music of the Whirling Dervishes is dominated by the haunting sound of the reed pipe or *ney* and can be heard in Konya during the Mevlana Festival each December.

FOLK DANCES

Each region in Turkey has its own special folk dance and costume, the best known of which are:

Horon   This Black Sea dance is performed by men only, dressed in black with silver trimmings. The dancers link arms and quiver to the vibrations of the *kemençe*, a kind of violin.

Kaşık Oyunu   The Spoon Dance is performed from Konya to Silifke and consists of gaily dressed male and female dancers clicking out the dance rhythm with a pair of wooden spoons in each hand.

Kılıç Kalkan   The Sword and Shield Dance of Bursa represents the Ottoman conquest of the city. It is performed by men only, dressed in early Ottoman battle dress. They dance to the sound of clashing swords and shields, without music.

Zeybek   In this Aegean dance colourfully dressed male dancers symbolize courage and heroism.

FOLK HEROES

Nasrettin Hoca was a thirteenth-century humorist and sage from Akşehir. His witticisms are known throughout Turkey and are often used to prove a point.

Karagöz is another jester, said to have lived in Bursa in the fourteenth-century and immortalized as a shadow puppet. Karagöz is a rough man of the people who uses his ribald wit to get the better of his pompous friend Hacivat. The puppets are made from gaily painted translucent animal skin and are projected onto a white screen.

Traditional Sports

Yağlı Güreş (grease wrestling) is the Turkish national sport, and every year in July wrestling championships are held in Kırkpınar, outside Edirne. The wrestling is made more difficult by the fact that the wrestlers smear themselves with oil.

Cirit Oyunu is game of dare-devil horsemanship where wooden javelins are thrown at horsemen of the opposing team to gain a point. The game is played mainly in Eastern Turkey.

Activities and Sports

From yachting and flottila sailing holidays to fishing, hunting, mountaineering, hiking and even pottery-making and carpet-weaving, Turkey offers a huge range of sporting and recreational possibilities.

YACHTING

Yachting and flottila sailing, in particular, are now well established, especially in prime holiday resorts such as Kuşadası, Bodrum and Marmaris, and a growing number of travel companies are now offering attractively priced arrangements for both the expert yachtsman and the novice.

The best season for sailing along the Aegean and Mediterranean coasts is between May and October. In winter the winds are frequently too gusty. In July to August for about twenty days the *meltem* (a NE wind) predominates in the Aegean Sea, mostly in the after-noons. Although the weather remains very fine and the sky is cloudless, the sea is very choppy. In addition, the sea breeze referred to as the *imbat* governs the length of the Aegean coast. The wind system is most moderate on the southern coast, which is partly sheltered from the *meltem*.

A meteorological bulletin in several languages is broadcast every day on the short-band (25 m.) from 07.30 to 08.00, and at 10.00, 12.00, 14.00 and 19.00 hrs.

Ports and Resorts　All ports of entry in Turkey are in a position to receive sailing boats all year round, and supplies such as food and motor fuel are usually fairly readily available. The marinas of Kuşadası and Bodrum, which are managed by the Tourism Bank of Turkey, as well as that of the holiday village of Altın Yunus at Çeşme, are open all year round and are fully equipped. The marinas of Kuşadası and Bodrum have a capacity of 310 and 125 craft respectively, although capacity at both marinas is being increased constantly to meet demand.

Facilities include connections for water and electricity and boat slipways (at Kuşadası).

Mooring   The coastline, especially between Izmir and Antalya, is much indented and comprises numerous coves and bays providing good mooring spots for sailing boats. The depths are generally from 10 to 12 m., and marine charts indicate the positions of dangerous reefs.

Forbidden Zones for Mooring
The entrance and exit of the Dardanelles, notably the Isles of Imroz and Bozca, the region of Kumkale, Mehmetçik Burnu and Anıt Körfezi
The zone north of the Bosphorus, the Gulf of Izmit and the Isle of Yassı (one of the Princes Islands)
Approaches to the port of Izmir, the port of Eski Foça to the south and the Isles of Uzun and Hekim
Certain parts of Mersin and Iskenderun

UNDERWATER DIVING
Underwater diving with oxygen tubes and underwater fishing are prohibited in Turkish waters.

HUNTING
Foreign hunters can only hunt in parties organized by Turkish travel agencies which have been authorized by the Ministry of Agriculture, Forestry and Rural Affairs. These agencies provide all information concerning seasons, authorized zones, formalities for permits, weapons and ammunition. A list of such agencies can be obtained from the Union of Travel Agencies (TURSAB), Cumhuriyet Cad. 187, Elmadağ, Istanbul.

FISHING
Tourists may fish for sporting purposes in non-prohibited regions without obtaining licences. Amateur equipment and non-commercial multi-hooked lines should be used, and nets should weigh not more than 5 kg. Commercial fishing by foreigners carries heavy

penalties. Details concerning fishing zones, the minimum size of fish that can be caught and the numbers of fish that can be caught per person can be obtained from the Department of Fisheries at the Ministry of Agriculture (Gıda – Tarım, Orman ve Köyişleri Bakanlığı, Su Ürünleri Genel Müdürlüğü, Ankara).

MOUNTAINEERING
Mountaineering is understandably becoming increasingly popular in Turkey, and although organized packages are still very much in their infancy, there's lots of scope for both the experienced and the amateur mountaineer.

In order to climb the Mount Ağrı and Cilo-Sat ranges, foreign mountainering groups must have special permission from the authorities concerned. For further information and contact with such Turkish groups, you can apply to the Turkish Mountaineering Club (Dağcılık Federasyonu, B.T.G.M., Ulus Işhanı, Λ-Blok, Ulus, Ankara, Tel. 10 85 66, ext. 356).

It is generally advisable to inform the Turkish Mountaineering Club of the region and time of the intended climb before the trip: the Club will then inform the relevant authorities in the region so that they will be prepared to assist should it be necessary.

For amateurs
Hasandağı (3,250 m.): situated to the south of Aksaray and accessible from all directions. The ideal starting points are Taşpınar on the Ankara–Adana road and the village of Helvadere in the Ihlara Valley.
Munzur Mountains: ranging from 3,300 m. to 2,500 m., this range lies between Elazığ and Erzincan. The highest peaks are north of Ovacık.
Erciyes Dağı (3,916 m.): this extinct volcano, the highest peak of Central Anatolia, lies to the south of Kayseri. The Tekir Yaylası (Plateau) is a recreation area in summer and a good skiing area in winter, and is reached via Hisarcık. The plateau is also the starting point for climbing the

peak from the north face (the climb up and back down takes about 10 to 11 hrs, and at the plateau is a 120-bed capacity chalet). Another route goes over the glacier called Sütdonduran (climbing pegs, pick axe and ropes are necessary).

Kaçkar Mountains: stretching for 30 km. running parallel to the Black Sea between Rize and Hopa, this range has peaks of up to 4,000 m. in height and has numerous glaciers, lakes, forests and hot springs. The mountains are divided into three groups: the Verşembek, the Kavrun and Altıparmak. One can reach any of the three groups via Ardeşen, a small town east of Rize, with accommodation facilities, and via Ayder. Base camp is generally set up on the Upper Kavrun at 2,750 m. altitude, and from there one can climb up to the Kaçkar peak at 3,932 m., the highest peak of the Kavrun group (7 to 8 hours up and back down). From the same base, one can climb up to Varoş (at 3,458 m., 6 to 7 hours up and down), and the Verşembek Peak (at 3,709 m., also 6 to 7 hours), both peaks being in the Verşembek group.

Another starting point is the village of Çat, reached via Çamlıhemşin. The Altıparmak group is accessible from the north via Ayder or Ardeşen, and then from the village of Dutha, or from the south coming from Erzurum via Tortum – where there are interesting waterfalls – and Karagöl. The highest peaks of the Karataş Mountains are more easily accessible from the south.

For experts

Aladağlar Mountains: situated 60 m. south of Niğde running in an east–west direction, the Valley of the Seven Lakes lies at 3,100 m. and is surrounded by high peaks. The ideal season for climbing is June to September, and the mountains are accessible via Niğde, Çamardı and Çukurbağ. Starting point for climbing the Demirkazık (3,756 m., up and back down in 9 to 10 hours) is Sokullupınar, about three hours' walk from Çukurbağ. Starting from the Valley of the Seven Lakes one can climb up to Kızılkaya (3,723 m., up and down in 10 hours), and

Direktaş (3,470 m., 10 hours). For climbing in the Kaldı Group, the highest peak of which is 3,734 m., the base camp should be made in the Sinekli Plateau.

Turasan Mountains: a continuation of the Aladağlar, with peaks such as Kızılyar (3,654 m.) and Turasan (3,499 m.)

Süphan Dağ (4,434 m.): the second highest peak in Anatolia, and with a crater lake. Starting from Adilcevaz, the trip to the top and back takes about three days.

Cilo-Sat Mountains: in this range are numerous glaciers, lakes and streams, so it is an ideal region for mountaineering and rambling. Best season for climbing and walking is June to September. Starting point is the high plateau of Mercan, five hours from Zap and 18 km. from Hakkari. Access to the Gelyaşım Peak (4,135 m.) is via the plateau of Serpil, and access to the Kisara Peak (3,752 m.) is via the village of Kursin. The track to the Samdi Peak and the surrounding glaciers starts from the Sat Govaruk Pasture. The glacier lake Bay Gölü, surrounded by alpine flora, lies at 2,700 m. altitude.

Ağrı Dağı: at 5,165 m., this is the highest mountain in Anatolia, with its peak totally capped by a glacier. Best season for the trip is June to September, and climbing pegs, pick axe and ropes are necessary. Doğubayazıt is the starting point, and the climb from the second camp up to the peak takes about eight hours. Another suitable starting point is Aralık.

Route plans and mountaineering guides are available from the information bureaux of the respective resorts.

SKIING

Turkey is not a noted winter sports destination, nor is it likely to become so in the near future. Facilities are, on the whole, not up to international standards, and access can often be a problem. However, the ski centres which are relatively easily accessible by road, or by Turkish Airlines domestic flights, and have adequate facilities for the winter sports enthusiast, are:

Bursa–Uludağ situated 36 km. south of Bursa, is accessible along a good road, or by cable-car. The ski area lies between 200–2,500 m., and the best skiing season is between January and April. Reasonably good accommodation is available in hotels and family chalets, with a total bed capacity of 3,100. At the resort are three chair-lifts, three ski-lifts, slalom and giant slalom courses and beginners' slopes. Ski equipment is available for hire.

Antalya–Saklıkent is situated north of Bakırlı Dağı, in the Beydağı mountain range 58 km. north of Antalya, at a height of 2,546 m. Accommodation is available in 2,500-bed capacity pensions/chalets, the best season being between January and April.

Bolu–Köroğlu situated on the Istanbul–Ankara highway 50 km. from Bolu, is surrounded by pinewoods. The ski area lies between 1,900 and 2,350 m. The 400-bed Kartal Hotel is of a reasonable standard, with facilities that include a swimming pool and ski-lift. Equipment can be hired, and ski instructors are available.

Erzurum–Palandöken, located 6 km. from Erzurum along a reasonably good road, lies at an altitude of 2,200 to 3,100 m. with some of the longest and most difficult courses – and best snow conditions – in Turkey. However, in order to ski here visitors must first obtain permission from the General Director of Physical Training (Beden Terbiyesi G.M. Kayak Federasyonu, Ulus İşhanı, A-Blok, Ulus, Ankara). Accommodation is available at a 100-bed capacity centrally heated ski lodge with telephone, restaurant, and chair-lift. Instruction and equipment are available. Accommodation is also available at a number of hotels in Erzurum. The best skiing times are between December and April.

Kars–Sarıkamış, located near Kars at an altitude of 2,250 m., also has good courses and ideal snow conditions. One can stay in the town itself or at the 60-bed capacity, centrally heated ski lodge with ski-lift and ski instructors available. Best season for skiing is between January and March.

Kayseri–Erciyes lies at an altitude of 2,150 m. on the eastern face of Erciyes Dağı at Tekir Yaylası (plateau), 25 km. from Kayseri. The skiing season is from November to May, and there is a 120-bed capacity ski lodge, good courses and snow. Instruction and equipment are available. However, like the ski centre at Erzurum–Palandöken, visitors wishing to use this centre must first obtain the permission of the General Directorate of Physical Training (for address, see above).

Youth and Student Travel

Holders of International Student Travel Conference (ISTC) cards, International Youth Hostel Federation cards, and those registered as 'student' or 'teacher' on their passports can benefit from the youth holiday opportunities available.

ACCOMMODATION
Topkapı Atatürk Student Center, Londra Asfaltı, Cevizli-bağ Durağı, Topkapı, Istanbul. Tel. 525 02 80 (girls' section), 525 50 32 – 523 94 88 (boys' section)
Kadırga Student Hostel, Cömertler Sokak No. 6, Kum-kapı, Istanbul. Tel. 528 24 80 – 523 24 81
Ortaköy Student Hostel for Girls, Palango Cad. No. 20, Ortaköy, Istanbul. Tel. 160 01 84 – 160 10 35 – 161 73 76
Intepe Youth and Boy Scout Hostel Güzelyalı Mevkil, Tusan Moteli Yanı, Guzelyalı 16, Çanakkale. Tel. 15 28 56 – 15 20 80
Hasanağa Youth and Boy Scout Hostel. Tel. Kumla 289
Cumhuriyet Youth Hostel, Cebeci, Ankara. Tel. 18 99 16 – 17 77 32

STUDENT REDUCTIONS
Some Turkish companies and organisations, such as Turkish Airlines, recognise the ISTC card and accordingly grant reductions to holders. Price reductions offered to students are:

Turkish Airlines: international flights 60 per cent; domestic flights 10 per cent
Turkish Maritime Lines: on international lines 15 per cent single, 25 per cent return; on domestic lines 50 per cent
Railways: 20 per cent
Museums: 50 per cent
Cinemas and concerts: 50 per cent.

TURKISH BATHS
Because of the emphasis placed on cleanliness by Islam, there have been public bath-houses (*hamam*) in Turkey since mediaeval times. There are separate baths for men and women or, when there is only one bath-house in the town, different days are allocated. After entering the hamam, and leaving your clothes in a cubicle, you proceed, wrapped in a towel (*peştemal*) to the *göbek taşı*, a large heated stone, to perspire and be rubbed down by a bath attendant. It's a very unusual experience! If the heat proves too much, you can retire to a cooler room for a while. This method of bathing is most refreshing, and many of the old marble baths are very interesting architecturally. Istanbul has some splendid bath-houses, the most interesting being Cağaloğlu Hamamı, Hilâliahmer Cad. (near the Blue Mosque), and Galatasaray Hamamı, Istiklâl Cad. Suterazi Sok. 24.

Miscellaneous Facts

Local time: GMT + 3 hrs.
Electricity: 220 volts a.c. throughout Turkey except for a small section of Istanbul. The voltage is clearly marked on all hotel power points.

Tap water: heavily chlorinated, and safe to drink in all cities

Weight and measures: metric system

Foreign newspapers: available in large cities the day after publication

Interpreters/guides: Ministry of Culture and Tourism bureaux and travel agents can provide professional interpreter-guides. Travel agents provide professional guides on all their tours.

Foreign language broadcasts in Turkey: the Third Programme of Turkish Radio and Television broadcasts programmes in Turkish, English, French and German on the Very Short Wave frequencies between 88 MHz and 99.2 MHz between 07.00 hrs. and 01.00 hrs. the following day.

A Brief History of Turkey

It is known that Turks lived in Dzungaria, to the north of East Turkestan, in 2000 BC. Unfortunately, there is no accurate and detailed information available about the Turkish states and the emperors of this era, the only limited sources being the historical documents of China, in which four Turkish emperors are named between the eighth and seventh centuries BC – Çun-Goey in 1766 BC, Tap-Pi in 1122 BC, Pe-Çi in 1116 BC, and Kio-Kue in 627 BC. Until the mid AD 1500s the Turkish states carried the names of the tribes which dominated the dynasty: for example, the Huns, Avars, Kırghız, Karluks and the Oghuz. In the mid 1500s Kök Turks began to rule all the Turkish tribes, creating a tendency for those people speaking Turkish to be referred to as Turks. The Chinese also adopted this name, and the neighbouring people called the Turks 'Tu-Kiu.' In time, and for a variety of reasons, the Turks began to leave their homeland and move to Iran, Caucasia, Anatolia, Eastern Europe and the Balkans.

Over a period Turks ruled in Asia, Eastern Europe and the northern and eastern coasts of Africa. And today, in addition to the Republic of Turkey, nearly 85 million people speak Turkish in an area extending from Yugoslavia in the west to China in the east.

THE GREAT HUN EMPIRE
The starting point of Turkish history is considered to be the Great Hun Empire. It was founded by Teoman

Yabgu, who united several Turkish tribes of his period, the Huns being descendants of the Kimmers and Sakas.

After Teoman Yabgu's death, his son, Mete, succeeded him, and during his reign the Turks invaded China and occupied an area extending from the northern coast of the Caspian Sea to the region that lies between Siberia and the Himalayas. Mete – who is known as Oghuz Khan in Turkish legend – also occupied parts of northern China, thereby extending the territory of his empire to 18 million sq. km. As a result of the political ploys of the Chinese, this great empire was divided into two: the south-eastern and north-western Hun empire. Under Chinese influence, and with their support and that of the Siyempis, the south-eastern Huns started feuding with the northern Huns. Losing their power entirely, the northern Huns dispersed in AD 93. The Siyempis grabbed sovereignity in the Southern Empire in AD 216, and the Huns finally migrated to Europe.

A section of the Huns who were forced to migrate to the West formed a state on the banks of the Volga under the administration of Balamir, and known as Volga Hun. It was short-lived. Most of the Huns, headed by Muncuh, crossed the Danube and settled in Hungaria in AD 375. They had occupied about seventy-five cities by 448, led by Muncuh's son Atilla, before reaching Istanbul. Atilla continued empire-building, conquering both Milan and Pavia, in Italy. But while he was marching towards Rome he was met by Pope Leon III and the Roman Consuls; he signed an agreement with them and returned home, dying one year later. After his death the European Hun Empire began to fall apart through massive power struggles, despite the efforts of Atilla's two sons Ilek and Dengizlik to keep the empire together.

Another branch of the Huns fled to the south and settled in a region covering Afghanistan, North India and part of Turkestan. The Akhun State was founded by Akhusunvar in AD 420 and became an empire during the reign of Toraman, who conquered the north of India in AD 496. The empire fell to the Kök Turks in AD 567.

KÖK TURKS (AD 552–745)

The Kök Turks occupy a special place in the history of the Turks because it was they who coined the term 'Turk' and who formed one of the major states of Turkish people. They overthrew the Avar dynasty in AD 552 and during their reign, which lasted for 193 years, they adopted the double-empire system: one of the founders of the empire, Bumin, became the Khan of the East and appointed his brother, Istemi, to the Khanate of the West. However, the political plotting of the Chinese contributed to the fall of the Kök Turk Empire. First the Eastern Empire came under the rule of the Chinese; and then in AD 647 it was totally annexed to the Chinese Empire. The West Kök Turk Empire retained its power and experienced a golden age during the reign of Ilteria Khan, who had assumed power in AD 682, but it gradually declined and the Ulgars became the dominant power.

AVARS OF EUROPE (AD 565–835)

The reason why the Avars migrated to the west and founded an empire in the territory where the Avars of Europe had lived a century previously is that the throne of the Great Turkish Empire had been passed on to the Kök Turks. Today's Ukraine, Hungary, Romania, Bulgaria, Czechoslovakia, Serbia and Croatia were within the frontiers of the empire. The Avars became increasingly powerful and beseiged Byzantium in AD 626. However, they were weakened by their unsuccessful siege, and were defeated by Charlemagne (AD 768–814) and his son Repin.

Charlemagne's domination of the Avars was very repressive. In the face of the powerful attacks by the Bulgarian Turks the empire disintegrated and the population resettled in Eastern Hungary and the Balkans, where they lost their native language, became Christian, and were assimilated.

CASPIANS (AD 468–865)

The empire which was founded by the Caspian Khans, descendants of the western branch of the Kök Turks, in Eastern Europe, maintained its sovereignity for more than five centuries, until defeated by the Russian prince Svetoslav. The Caspians, who survived until the eleventh century as a small principality, were completely assimilated by such newcomers as Oghuz, Kipchak and Pechnek Turks.

UYGURS (AD 745–940)

Kutlug Bilge Khan overthrew the Kök Dynasty in AD 745 and became the Great Turkish Khan. As a result, the Uygurs, who were living in the confederation as a kingdom, became the dominant power.

After the murder of Uge Khan in AD 845 the Uygurs achieved a high degree of civilization, and made Karabalgasun their capital. The Uygur Empire was reduced to a kingdom when the Karaman Dynasty dominated the Khanate after AD 940, although it survived until 1260, when the Uygurs were assimilated by the Mongols.

KARAHANLILIAR (AD 940–1040)

The Karahanlılıar, who ascended to the throne of the Great Turkish Khanate in AD 940, reigned in Central Asia, and the adoption of Islam by Satuk Bugra Khan led the way for Turks to accept Islam at the time when its influence was waning. Thus the Turks played an important role in the Islamic world in the ensuing years. The Turks moved from Central Mongolia during the reign of the Karahanlılıar, who fell from power in 1040.

GHAZNAVIDS (AD 962–1187)

The Ghazna State was formed by Alp Tekin, who was appointed Governor of Horasan during the period of the Samanoğulları Emperor Abdulmelik, and it occupied an area of nearly 5 million sq. km., extending through Afghanistan, the Caspian coast, Iran and North India. The Ghaznavids experienced their most powerful and brilliant years during the period of Sultan Mahmoud, but lost their sovereignity between 1072 and 1187 to the Seljuks, who represented the Great Turkish Khanate. They were utterly destroyed by the Gurs in 1187.

THE GREAT SELJUK EMPIRE (AD 990–1157)
The Seljuks originate from the Kınık branch of the Uçoklar tribe of the Oghuz Turks, who were dominant in the administration of the Turks when the Seljuks were entering the scene. The Seljuks took power in 990, first occupying Merv and subsequently conquering Nishapur. The Seljuks defeated the Ghaznavids at the Battle of Dandenekan, and Tuğrul Bey (1040–63) became Khan. He was succeeded in 1063 by his cousin Alparslan, who set about decreasing the pressure of the Byzantine Empire on the Anatolian Turks, with the result that it was shaken both economically and militarily. Byzantine Emperor Romanos Diogenes formed an army of 250,000 troops in order to end this attack, but was defeated by the 50,000 troops of Alparslan in 1071. After this victory the Turks began to pour into Anatolia. Alparslan was murdered in 1072, and his son Melik Şah (1072–92) replaced him. Melik Şah enlarged the territory of the empire from the Tanrı Mountains to the Marmara Sea and the Mediterranean, and from the Caucasus to Yemen and the Gulf. He conquered Jerusalem in 1076, Antakya in 1085 and Urfa in 1087.

In 1077 Melik Şah gave Anatolia to his uncle, Süleyman Şah, on condition that Anatolia be affiliated to his empire. Thus Süleyman Şah took his place in history as the Conqueror of Anatolia and the founder of the Anatolian Seljuk Empire.

After the death of Melik Şah, struggles for the throne combined with the attack of Crusaders began to weaken the empire, and despite a resurgence during the period of Sultan Sancar, it was dispersed upon the latter's death in 1157.

169

ANATOLIAN SELJUK EMPIRE (1077–1308)

The Anatolian Seljuk Empire developed in a very short period, having spread its sovereignity throughout Anatolia by the time Süleyman Şah died in 1086. Meanwhile, the Crusaders posed a tremendous threat. The First Crusaders' Army (1096–9) looted Anatolian settlements on its way to Jerusalem, while the Second and Third Crusades (1147–9 and 1189–92 respectively) also managed to cross into Anatolia, despite heavy losses. However, the Crusaders' occupation was halted, and the Anatolian Seljuk Empire continued to develop rapidly, reaching its peak during the reign of Sultan Alaeddin Keykubat (1219–37). It was he who conquered Alaiye (today's Alanya), and gave it his name. His successor, Giyaseddin Keyhüsrev II, was not so successful, and the death knell of the Seljuk Empire was sounded at the Battle of Kösedağı, which was won by the Mongols.

HARZEMŞAHLAR (1157–1231)

Mohammed Harzem-Şah founded the State of Harzemşahlar in Gürgenç, which he pronounced capital of the state, after the death of the Emperor of the Great Seljuk Empire, Sultan Sancar, in 1157. The Eastern Turkish Khanate was assumed by the Harzemşahlar when the Seljuks of Iraq dispersed in 1914. The Harzemşahlar moved their capital to Samarkand, but were weakened in 1220 by the Mongol occupation which started during the reign of Kutbeddin, who was unsuccessful against the armies of Genghis Khan.

TURK-MONGOL EMPIRE

After the migration of the Turks to the west, the Mongols – who were originally from Altaic tribes, as were the Turks – formed their state in Central Asia. The empire established sovereignity in Central Asia and began to expand. Its founder, Temuçin, marched on the North Chinese Empire in 1211 and conquered Peking in 1215; and in the ensuing years the Mongols extended their sovereignity to Anatolia. During the reign of Genghis Khan the empire covered the whole of Asia, while on his death in 1227 it was divided into four: China Mongols (Kubilay Dynasty), Iran Mongols (Ilhanlılar), Central Asia Mongols (Çağatay) and Kipchak Mongols (Altinordu). In time the Kubilay Dynasty was assimilated by the Chinese and the other three survived under the name of the Turk-Islam Empire, after adopting the Islamic religion.

TAMERLANE EMPIRE (1369–1501)

The childhood of Tamerlane, who gave his name to the empire, coincides with a period of continuous battles between Mongol khans and beys. Tamerlane allied himself to Kazgan Khan, and continued to fight after Kazgan's murder. And after defeating the Çağatay Emperor he proclaimed himself 'emir' (leader, ruler, prince) of the Mongols and Turks at the Convention in Samarkand in 1369. He destroyed the Altinordu State in 1395 and conquered Iran, Eastern Anatolia and Baghdad; changed his route to conquer the northern part of India; and returned to loot Anatolia and defeat the Ottoman Khan Yıldırım Bayezid at the Battle of Ankara in 1402. Tamerlane died in 1403 while preparing to march on China, and the country was weakened as a result of the ensuing squabbles for the division of the throne among his sons and grandchildren. The empire was destroyed by the Saybanis in 1501.

BABUR EMPIRE (1526–1858)

Babur, the son of the emperor of Fergana and the founder of the empire, conquered Kabul after his father's death in 1494; twenty yeras later, he marched to the south again and conquered Lahore in 1524 and Delhi and Agra after the Battle of Panipat in 1526. Subsequently, the Babur Empire occupied the regions of Gucarat, Bengal, Kashmir, Orisa, Berar and Kandes, but was considerably weakened by rebellions. During the reign of Shah Alem (1759–1806) the British Trading Company moved into

171

India and began to administer the Bengal, Bihar and Orisa regions. In 1858 the company handed over the administration to Britain, thus ending the Babur Empire.

OTTOMAN EMPIRE (1281–1922)

The Ottoman Empire reigned over three continents for more than six centuries. Its core was the Karacahisar region, which was given to Ertuğrul Bey by Alaeddin Keykubat and subsequently inherited by Ertuğrul Bey's son Osman, who enlarged the territory considerably. On his death in 1324 he was succeeded by his son Orhan bey, who continued his father's expansionist policies. He moved the capital of the state to Bursa after conquering that city in 1326, and three years later conquered Iznik (Nicaea) – a move which caused great repercussions in Europe and the Near East in view of Iznik's importance as a Christian centre.

The Ottoman Empire continued to grow, occupying an area of 95 thousand sq. km. by the time of Orhan Ghazi's death in 1362, when his son Sultan Murad I assumed the throne. Conquests followed one after the other, in quick succession, so that by 1389, the empire had spread over 500 thousand sq. km.

Murad I was succeeded by Yıldırım (the Thunderbolt) Bayezid who, after uniting all the Anatolian beylicates and maintaining political unity, continued to enlarge the territory of the Ottoman Empire in Rumeli, successfully beating off a challenge by an army of European troops under the command of the King of Hungary. Mehmet II (1451–81) continued the march forward, and conquered Istanbul in 1453, a victory which saw the start of a major phase of development for the Ottoman Empire that lasted until the end of the sixteenth century.

In 1520 the empire was ruled by Süleyman (also known as Suleiman or Solyman), described in the West as 'the Magnificent' and in the East as 'Kanuni' (the Lawgiver). During his reign, which lasted forty-six years, the Ottomans conquered Belgrade and Rhodes. Taking stock of the situation in Europe, Süleyman left aside his father's policy oriented to the east and concentrated, instead, on the west. He defeated the Hungarian Army at the Battle of Mohacs in 1526 and conquered Budin (Budapest), and later Baghdad. The Grand Admiral of the Ottoman Fleet, Barbarossa Hayreddin Pasha, seized Libya, Morocco and Algeria, and in 1538 won a notable victory in Preveza, defeating the emperor's forces commanded by Admiral Andrea Doria.

The total area of the empire was 15 million sq. km. when Süleyman died in his battle tent at Szigetvar in 1566. With his death the heroic age of Ottoman history came to an end, although the expansion of Ottoman territory continued. Nevertheless, the Ottoman empire was entering a period of stagnation and decline, while the Renaissance was just beginning in Europe. The Sultans succeeding Süleyman (Selim II, Murad II, Mehmet III, Ahmed I) were unsuccessful in improving matters. The war declared against the German King in 1593 ended with an agreement under which Germany was able to exact various concessions from the Sultan, such as not paying annual taxes, and having the title 'Holy Roman Empire' accepted by the Ottomans.

During the reign of Murad IV (1623–40), who became Sultan after the murder of reformist Sultan Osman II, measures were taken to restore the empire: these didn't succeed, and the decline could not be halted.

In the early eighteenth century, war was declared on Russia on the advice of King Charles XII of Sweden. The Russian Army was encircled in the Pruth, but the Ottomans failed to take full advantage of the situation, and in the Treaty of the Pruth in 1711, the Russians saved their army and the Ottomans took back the Azak stronghold. This incident was succeeded by the Conquest of Morea in 1715, from the Venetians. Austria entered the war, and the Ottoman army was defeated in the Battle of Petervaradin.

It wasn't until the nineteenth century that the Ottoman administrators realized that the western states were advancing by attaching great importance to industriali-

173

zation and education. But the attempts of Selim III (1789–1807) and Mahmoud II (1808–39) to make drastic changes were insufficient to save the empire. It was a turbulent period, embracing the five-year Turco-Russian war, the Greek and Serbian uprising, and the Crimean War.

The wars between the Ottomans and the Russians (1877–78) were brought to an end by the Treaties of Ayastefanos (San Stefano) and Berlin. Under these, Serbia, Romania and Karadag declared their independence, and Bulgaria became a self-governing principality. Several Turkish cities on the eastern frontiers were ceded to the Russians.

During the First World War the Ottoman Empire suffered a loss of 400,000 casualties and, being defeated by the Allies, signed an armistice at Mondros in 1918. Following this they were forced to sign the Sèvres Treaty in 1920 which aimed at dividing the lands of the empire. The Turkish nation – in protest at the Mondros Armistice and the Sèvres Treaty – started its War of Independence under the command of Mustafa Kemal Atatürk. After the victory, the Turkish Grand National Assembly in Ankara abolished the office of the Sultan on 1 November, 1922, ending 631 years of Ottoman rule, and founded the Turkish Republic.

TURKISH REPUBLIC (1922–)

Enormous changes have occurred within Turkish society since then, and despite the violence and political unrest of the 1970s, culminating in the Armed Forces stepping in to prevent civil war in 1980, Turkey is now on course to becoming a full democracy.

Martial law has been lifted in the majority of the country's 67 provinces, and modern-day Turkey is a nationalist, democratic and secular state, based on the rule of law and social justice, with sovereignity exercised through the elected Turkish Grand National Assembly.

Executive power is exercised by the President of the Republic and the Council of Ministers, and Turkey is a member of NATO, OECD and the Council of Europe, and is an associate member of the EEC.

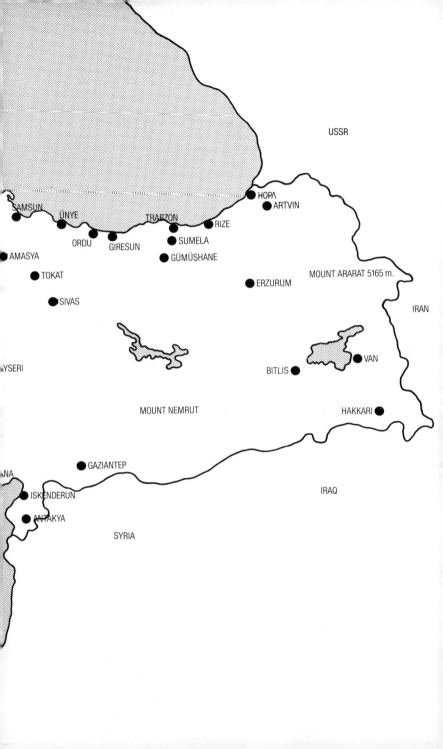